The Art of
Redesign

5 Simple Steps to
No-Cost Redecorating

Val Sharp CRSS, CISS

Certified Redesign and Staging Specialist

The Art of Redesign
5 Simple Steps to No-Cost Redecorating
By Val Sharp

Editor: Jim Osborne, Victoria, BC; Michael Kaye, www.begin2write.com
Copyeditor: Christine Frank, www.ChristineFrank.com
Cover and Interior Design: Wendy Brookshire, Toolbox Creative, www.ToolboxCreative.com

Val Sharp
The Art of Redesign: 5 Simple Steps to No-Cost Redecorating
ISBN: 978-0-9808835-0-3
Publication Year 2008

This book is available for special promotions and premiums. For details contact the author at vsharp@shaw.ca

This book is dedicated to the special group of volunteers from the Canadian Redesigners Association (www.canadianredesigners.org) and Interior Redesign Industry Specialists (www.WeRedesign.com) who selflessly dedicate their time and talent to creating havens for healing across North America for women living with ovarian cancer.

Ovarian cancer is the disease that whispers. Find out the symptoms: www.ovariancanada.org and www.ovarian.org

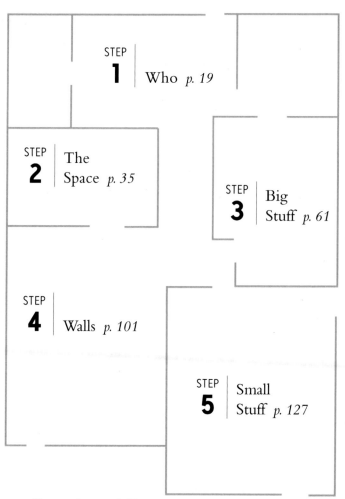

Foreword

When I first met Val Sharp, I didn't realize how much I would learn from her. After all, I'd been running my professional organizing business for several years and was hosting a hit television show. However, being a life-long learner, I'm always open to adding new skills to my toolbox, so I took her five-day course. Wow! What an experience.

In her warm, friendly style, Val taught me how to transform a house into a home with little or no money. She is not only a talented redesigner, but a person who truly cares about creating homes that people love. I don't know who was more excited about the makeovers we did — the homeowners or us.

In *The Art of Redesign*, Val takes you back to basics and shows you how you can truly have a home that works for you and your family, without buying anything new – what a concept! Just by following her five easy steps, you too can have a home you love right now.

Everything I learned in Val's five-day course is packed into this easy-to-read book. The inclusion of real client stories and photos brings the concepts to life and makes them easy to understand.

Written in a conversational style, the book is nicely laid out and easy to understand. The before and after pictures are clear and dramatic — and who doesn't love a great reveal! Not only will this book teach you how to redesign, it will also help you understand what it is and how much impact it can have in all areas of your life.

As a personal coach, I really appreciate the coach in Val as she tells her inspiring stories from redesign experiences. Redesign is not just about decorating. It's about highlighting the things you love in your home, and making it functional for the people who live there. Yes, your rooms will look beautiful, but more importantly, your rooms will feel so good you won't want to leave them.

I would recommend this book to any do-it-yourselfers who want to use what they have so they can save money, save the environment and express their creativity.

If you care about your home, and recognize the important role your environment plays in the health and well-being of all who live there, read this book. It could change your life.

Hellen Buttigieg
Certified Professional Organizer, Life Coach and TV Personality

Introduction

With the increase in emphasis on homes, we are bombarded with messages telling us that what we have isn't good enough. We need to buy different, new and up-to-date. In magazines we are told we need to buy new furniture, new accessories, and new window treatments. Television shows make us believe we have to do entire renovations in order to love our homes. Advertisements everywhere promote buying new in order to have a home of which we can be proud.

So we go shopping. And we buy new furniture at vast expense; we buy new lamps, new artwork, and new accessories. And at the end of all that spending, we still don't love our homes. Something still isn't right.

The reason? We haven't paid attention to the basics of what makes a home beautiful. Our real objective is to give ourselves a warm, inviting home that meets our needs and the needs of the other people who live there. And here's a novel thought: we don't need to buy anything new.

Creating a home you love is not about decorating. It's about creating a space that works for you and highlighting the possessions that you love. The focus is on you and the other people who live in the home and how you would like to use your space. It's all about what would make it special for you, not what would look good in a decorating magazine.

In this book I will walk you through the basic steps to create a home you love. I will teach you the techniques I have learned as a professional redesigner, and I will teach you a system of layering furniture, art, and accessories to create beauty wherever the eye looks. You will learn to use your furnishings so your home works for the people who live there. You will learn to create balance and flow in your rooms. You will learn the power of hanging art to work with the furniture, and you will learn to accessorize to enhance the art and the furnishings.

Redesign is the art of making over your home using your existing furnishings. When I began my career as a redesigner, I thought it was about making people's homes pretty. The concept of creating something beautiful from what people already owned was intriguing to me.

What came as a huge shock to me when I started redesigning homes for people was the enormous emotional impact that my redesigns had on my clients.

One woman, a couple months after the redesign, said, "I can't tell you how it's changed my life. I even care what I wear now."

Denise, a single mother, confided to me that she hadn't wanted to get out of bed in the morning for two years. After the redesign, she jumped out of bed with excitement. Moreover, her teenage children were keeping the house clean because they wanted to keep the feeling I had created.

> "The changes you brought about in our house have everyone who comes in here impressed. It's so much cozier and friendly and I love the front room especially. The best part is that the kids and I are keeping it cleaner now that we like it ... For once I have a list of things I'd like to buy that has some purpose ... you have a real talent and this job will bring so many people happiness."
>
> Denise Gibson, Teacher, Port Moody, BC

I was even more amazed at the reaction of younger people. They always tell you exactly what they think. One client's six-year-old boy walked into the room, looked at his parents, and said, "Don't change it back!" And his ten-year-old sister said, "It's like walking into a picture."

A typical teenage boy walked into the family room we'd redesigned and said, "The energy is different in here." His mother said she didn't even think he'd notice anything, never mind the energy in the room.

Two young boys came home and were bouncing off the walls with excitement after we'd done the redesign. "Mom, come here! Dad, look at this!"

In another home, a five-year-old girl started to cry when she was told we hadn't been hired to redesign her bedroom. She wanted her bedroom to be as wonderful as the rest of the home.

People would come home to their 'new' house and jump up and down in glee, or tears would well up in their eyes as they took in the beautiful space created with their own possessions. I watched their bodies relax as they felt the peace in their 'new' home envelop them.

At first I thought they just liked how their home looked. But over time I realized that it had less to do with how the home looked and more to do with how it felt. The feelings of balance, harmony, and peace that people felt when they walked into their warm, inviting space released enormous joy and serenity.

What I gradually came to realize was that a redesigned home took them to that place every time they walked through their front door. And this is what redesigning your home will do for you.

Through this book, you will come to shape a home that you love. You really will.

Val Sharp
Victoria, BC

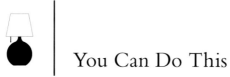

You Can Do This

Some people who pick up this book may think they haven't the talent or creativity to redesign their home. If you're one of them, you may be interested in my journey to discovering my creative side.

When I first decided to take my redesign training, I was scared. I had never been a particularly 'creative' person. In fact, in school I was told that I wasn't artistic. I excelled in math so I became a chartered accountant, working with a large corporation. But I was constantly drawn to the graphics, pictures, and writing in the annual reports I produced. Over many years, many jobs, and many careers, I managed to evolve my work into more creative fields like multimedia and communications.

THE LEAP

Then I discovered redesign. Finally, I had found my passion. I read books and searched the Internet for courses so I could train in this profession. There were no courses being offered in Canada at the time but I discovered a woman who offered a course in San Francisco. She had been redesigning homes for over ten years and was a founding member of a redesign organization in the U.S. I took the giant leap and signed up.

The entire time I spent at the course, my inner voice told me that I wasn't creative, that I couldn't do this, and that only 'artistic' people could do it. After all, the artistic people were the ones who went into interior design.

During the course I began to realize I had a flair for furniture placement and even how to hang art, but accessorizing eluded me.

It seemed like everyone else could accessorize a tabletop in about three minutes and it looked great. I, on the other hand, would walk around with an ornament in my hand for ages. I would put it down somewhere and it wouldn't look right. So I'd pick it up and wander some more, then try putting it down somewhere else. Everywhere I put it, it looked wrong. I felt lost, as if I were traveling in a foreign country and didn't know the language. I was convinced I would never 'get it.'

PRACTICE...

Every night I went back to my friend's apartment in San Francisco and practiced in her home, accessorizing and re-accessorizing everything she owned. (She was very patient with me, but did ask me to return some of the furniture and accessories to her bedroom before I left, as she needed to use them!) When I finished the course I still felt pretty insecure about my abilities. Could I do this?

Returning home to Victoria I began going to networking events and talking about my business. I met a woman interested in the concept who really wanted her home redesigned. I negotiated a redesign of her home in exchange for a 'marketing coffee party.' She would invite all her friends over after the redesign, and I would show up with cake and cookies to discuss it with them. We would also show them the 'before' photos so they could see the transformation. I decided this was a great way to start marketing my business, and also get a testimonial and some 'before and after' photos for my portfolio.

Imagine my dismay when I walked into her condo and it looked fabulous.

"Are you sure you want me to do this?" I asked her (thinking that I wasn't going to get very dramatic 'before and after' photos.) "Your place looks great."

"Oh yes," she said." I just want a change."

I looked at her, looked at her beautiful home, and said "Well, I'm not sure I can make it look better, but I can definitely make it look different."

...MAKES PERFECT

The day of the big redesign arrived. I had met a woman who was a friend of a friend and asked her if she would consider being my assistant. When you do a redesign of a home, you need someone to help you move furniture around and hang art. You also want someone you can brainstorm with. This is critical because of what I call the "exponential creativity" effect. This is how it works. If I have an idea, it ends there. However, if I have someone to bounce that idea off, they can come up with a further idea, which can spark another idea in me, which then sparks another idea in them, and on it goes. The end result is that the creativity is multiplied exponentially.

Back to the redesign. My new assistant and I went to work.

We followed the system and guidelines I'd learned and at the end of the day were astounded at the results. Magic had happened! The space wasn't just better, it was light-years better! I couldn't believe it. Everywhere we looked in the room, we saw a beautiful vignette (a French term which means tableau or composition, often used in redesign when describing a beautiful corner in a home that looks like a work of art). The home was cozier, friendlier, and beautiful, all at the same time.

My assistant turned to me and said, "You're so good at accessorizing." I started to laugh. I was creative!

But how would the client react to what we'd done? I held my breath as she walked in. She put her hands over her face and said, "Oh my god, I can't believe this is my home."

A week later she sent me the following testimonial:

"I love it. I absolutely love it! I was stunned ... I was pleased ... It all looks so good. I didn't think it could look so different (and better) using exactly what I had."

— Linden Michael, Travel Counselor, Blaney's Travel, Victoria, BC

From that auspicious beginning, I never looked back. I now train people in starting their own interior redesign business.

I now know that I am creative.

And I'm willing to bet that you are too.

WHY IT'S WORTH THE TROUBLE

Having a home that you love is priceless. It's the best gift you can give yourself. You will love to come home to it. You will feel more comfortable. Every day you will feel a little lift as your eyes move around the room and fall on the things you love, highlighted in unique ways. Your home will be your retreat. And you will be proud to invite people to visit and discover what it says about you.

You don't need to buy anything new to have this feeling of abundance in your home. Just follow the simple steps in this book. However, if you do decide to buy something new later on, you'll have set the foundation. You'll know exactly what you need to buy, how big it should be, what color will work, and where it will go. So you won't make costly mistakes buying things that don't work.

Following is a brief description of the five basic steps to redesigning a home. In the next five chapters I will show you how to apply them to your own home. I recommend reading the entire book quickly. As ideas for your home come to you, just make a note of them and carry on. When you've finished reading the book, you can then go back and follow the steps to actually do the work in your home.

STEP 1 – WHO

In Step 1 we take a close look at who lives in the home and what their needs are. You need to be clear about what you love, what's not working, and how you want to use your space before you start changing things. What function does the room serve? Who are the people who live there? What are their needs? What special treasures do you want to highlight? We'll show you how to examine these things so you can create a home that truly works.

STEP 2 – THE SPACE

Step 2 talks about clearing the space — taking all the furniture out so you can start from scratch. This will give you a 'clean-slate' perspective of the space. It also provides you with the most opportunities for furniture placement. This is the most important step in the process. Once the room is clear you can better see the architectural lines and features of your home, and begin to work with them — a step ignored by most people. When you work with the architectural lines of the home it gives the room harmony.

STEP 3 – BIG STUFF

In Step 3 we look at placing the furniture: "the big stuff," to create balance and harmony in the room. This is critical. If the furniture isn't properly placed, then no amount of art and accessories will make the room feel better. Over and over I see people buy more art, buy more accessories, and buy more furniture, all in an effort to make their homes feel and look right. And it never works. The reason? The furniture placement is wrong. Once the furniture placement is right, then everything else follows.

STEP 4 – WALLS

Step 4 is about hanging the art and bringing color and life into the room. So many homes have art that is hung too high. We'll show you how to determine the right height for your art so it works with the furniture. I also see homes where art is hung randomly, just to fill up space on the wall. The result is that the art looks cheap and doesn't have the impact on the viewer that it should. It also makes the room feel disjointed. We want your art to shine, to work with the furniture and accessories so that everything in the room looks beautiful and feels cohesive.

STEP 5 – SMALL STUFF

Step 5 talks about accessories: those small things that pack a big punch. Most of us aren't happy with our rooms, so we buy more accessories. When that doesn't work, we add more accessories. We also think that everything we own must be on display at all times. In this chapter we'll look at how to display only the treasures we love. And we'll show you how to display them so that they take center stage. The big surprise is that you don't have to get rid of things you love. You can display a lot of treasures and the room will still feel calm — if you know how to do it properly.

Ready to begin? Now let's apply these five steps to your home.

Throughout the next five chapters I'll highlight each of the steps with stories from my own experiences in redesigning many of the homes I've done.

STEP
1 | Who

In Step 1 we take a close look at who lives in the home and what your needs are. Sometimes the home can be totally at odds with who lives there and their needs. Let me give you an example of just that.

STORIES
from Redesign

Carol was a divorced woman who lived in a large city in a downtown high-rise apartment with a fabulous view of the water.

Carol's living room/dining room was one large space. You first walked into the dining room and then the living room was behind it.

She had a traditional dining room suite, and her living room furniture was lined up along the walls. Her place felt so lonely. The furniture arrangement was designed for a family or couple to live there, not a single person. When we went into her bedroom, it was just sad. When lying in her bed, she looked at a huge wall that had one small piece of art hanging in the middle. In my opinion, this is a sure-fire way to get depressed.

When I asked her how she entertained, she said that her friends came over for drinks and appetizers and then they went out for dinner. She had a dining room table and china cabinet so I asked her when she used it. She replied that she sat at the table to watch TV in the morning and eat her breakfast.

Carol was a successful career woman. She was intelligent, energetic, and fashionably dressed. The woman and her home had nothing in common with each other. Her home still reflected her old, married life, but how she dressed and lived reflected her new, single life. We needed to fix this disconnect.

The first thing we did was to flip the room. We put the 'living room' first so that when you walked into the space, you were welcomed with a lovely, inviting conversation area looking out over the water. Behind that, we put the dining room table and her TV so she could still sit at her table to watch TV and eat her breakfast. The good news was that now she could also take in the view of the water at the same time, and sit in the morning sun that comes in through that window.

We then took the top off her china cabinet and left it as a hutch in the 'living room' with a couple of beautiful pieces of art over it and a lamp on one end. This made a fabulous serving area for entertaining. It also eliminated the traditional 'dining room suite' which implied that a family should live there, not a hip, successful single woman.

For her bedroom, we put the top of the china cabinet on the floor of the bedroom as a place for books and some favorite ornaments. With a couple pieces of art over the cabinet, that big, blank wall was now a warm, inviting space. We also moved a wing-back armchair, a plant, a lamp, and a table into her bedroom. We placed these by the window so she could look at her view of the city and read a book or have a glass of wine. Instead of a lonely place to go to bed at night, her bedroom was now a cozy haven from the stresses of the world.

This redesign was particularly exciting for me because we gave her a home that was a reflection of her — and her new life. I could visualize her enjoying her new space with her friends and loving her home even while she was alone. Instead of a feeling of "I used to have a family and now I don't," it felt like "I'm a trendy single woman who has a full, vibrant life."

Imagine what that change in viewpoint can do for someone's perspective on life!

BEFORE: *The traditional china cabinet didn't reflect the trendy woman who lived here.*

BEFORE: *The furniture arrangement ignored the beautiful views of the city and the water.*

BEFORE: *Furniture was lined up along the walls, making the room feel cold and sterile.*

AFTER: *By removing the top of the china cabinet, we created a buffet that was more contemporary. It was also more functional, as it could be used for serving appetizers.*

AFTER: *The new furniture arrangement created a cozy conversation area for guests that incorporated the great view. We also highlighted her favorite sculpture. The dining room table was positioned so that she could have her breakfast, watch the news, and look at the water.*

AFTER: *The top of the china cabinet wasn't wasted. We used it in her bedroom to warm up the space and give her a place for her cherished books.*

YOUR OWN HOME

Your home is very personal. You need to take all your wants and needs into account: your likes and dislikes and how you use your home. It's about creating a home you will love. You need to focus on what you will love and create that environment for yourself. The bottom line is that you will feel better about yourself and your furnishing selections and you will enjoy living in the space.

You will be shocked at how beautiful your home can be by just using the items that already exist there. It's all in how you place things, how everything works together, and the balance, harmony, and flow in the home.

YOUR GOALS

1. The first goal is to highlight your possessions. This means leaving space around your furniture to show it off, hanging your art to its best advantage, and displaying your treasures so you can appreciate them. It is fundamentally about honoring/validating the choices you have made over the years.

2. The second goal is to incorporate as many of your 'wish list' items as you possibly can. Would you like a reading chair in the family room? Do you want a spot to do your arts and crafts? Do you have a favorite TV-watching chair that needs to be placed facing the TV?

3. The third goal of a redesign is to incorporate as many of your possessions as possible while still having a functional, harmonious, warm, inviting home. As in traditional design, the foundational principle of redesign is "function first." You never sacrifice the use of the room in order to make it look pretty.

ASSESSING YOUR NEEDS

The design of your home impacts everything in your life: how you approach life, how you feel in your home, and how proud of your home you feel. Redesign can have far-reaching emotional effects on your whole outlook toward life.

It is imperative to understand how you want to use the space, as it will impact all of your redesign decisions. You need to ascertain what you like and dislike, how you use the space, how many people need to see the TV, the feel you want the space to have, and any sentimental pieces that need to be highlighted.

BEFORE: *This client was always bringing in extra seating when she had guests over because her conversation area was too small. However, she had a loveseat and chair that was never used in the back corner of the room.*

AFTER: *We gave her a larger conversation area by adding the loveseat. We also highlighted her favorite table and gave her a lovely place to have tea or play bridge. The large carpet needed to be replaced but the thought of it was overwhelming for her. We rolled it up and put it in the garage, then used her carpet from the dining room as an area rug. The dining room was beautiful without it. We saved her the cost of a new rug.*

COMMON THREAD

Most homes can be made to work. When we buy things, there is usually a common thread in them. This common thread seems to be there throughout our lives. We may buy the same colors, shapes, or materials. The result is that the items in the home usually work together so you often don't have to buy anything new. You just need to look for the common threads.

ASCERTAIN YOUR PRIORITIES

The whole point of this exercise is to design your home to work for you. How many people live there? How do you entertain? Does anyone have specific hobbies that need to be taken into account? Are there any other special needs the family has?

Also, it's your home, so you want to be surrounded by things you love. I highly recommend getting rid of anything you don't love or that isn't useful to you. Give it away to people who will love it or use it; sell it and use the money to buy those items that are missing from your home; or just throw it away. But don't have it displayed in your home.

BEFORE: *This client had a space off the kitchen that served as both a dining room and a living room. Both spaces were small and crowded. Then there was this room right beside the kitchen which had a loveseat and a piano. They rarely used this room with its beautiful fireplace.*

AFTER: *In order to better use the space in their home, we moved the dining room to the space previously occupied by the loveseat and piano. This allowed us to create a huge living room with more seating (because of the extra loveseat) and a piano — much more functional.*

THINK OUTSIDE OF THE BOX

Look at your family's needs and try things that work for them. Perhaps you always eat in the kitchen, even when you're entertaining. If your dining room only gets used once a year for the holidays, maybe it doesn't make any sense to have a separate dining room. What else could that room be? Maybe it could be a quiet reading room with a couple of big, cozy chairs and reading lamps, or an arts and crafts room, or maybe you could move your office out of your bedroom and create an office in that space previously occupied by the dining room table.

Maybe you use your small dining room frequently for large dinner parties and your large living room is seldom used. Why not switch them? How wonderful to be able to dine by the fireplace! And the small room that used to be the dining room? Turn it into a cozy room to read, watch TV, or entertain a few guests for drinks. All that's required is moving the chandelier and the furniture.

What about the living room that is never used? Many people have family rooms or great-rooms where everyone congregates while their living room sits idle. Even when guests come over, they don't go in the living room. Perhaps that space could be better used another way. If you look at how you use your home, you may decide that the large living room should be the family room and the small family room should be the living room. Or maybe for the way you entertain, a giant pool table in the middle of the room would be perfect. It's all about you.

SHOPPING IN YOUR HOME

Shopping in your home starts when you are looking at how you use the rooms and continues through the whole redesign process.

You need to constantly be on the lookout for that one piece that's just what you need when you're redesigning a room. For example, when you're redesigning your living room, you'll be asking yourself the following questions:

* Is the area rug the right one for the room? Does it need to be switched with one from another room?

* Do any of the large pieces need to be switched with those in another room? Sofas? Chairs? Coffee table?

* Are there any furniture pieces in the basement/garage/storage or other rooms that would work? What about art in other rooms? Should it be here instead?

Consider your whole home a wealth of objects that you can access at no cost to make just the special room you need.

Let me give you an example of shopping the home.

STORIES
from Redesign

After discussion with Katie, we decided to change her living room into a 'hangout' for her teenagers. They had been using the space for that purpose anyway and she had a beautiful great-room that was perfect for her 'adult' living room.

The new 'hangout' was the first room people saw when they walked into the home so it still had to look good. We kept the dark grey sofas that were in the room as they were comfortable and the right color for constant use. We moved the brightly colored, expensive carpet into the great-room where the colors worked better and she didn't have to be concerned about it being damaged. We found a brown and grey carpet in the foyer that worked perfectly with the furniture in the teenage 'hangout'.

Next we angled the furniture so that it guided visitors past the room and through to the colorful great-room which was now the 'adult' room.

The homeowner was a painter and had some gorgeous huge pieces of black and grey art in the great-room and the foyer. We moved these to the 'hangout' where they looked incredible with the black-and-grey TV and dark grey furniture. This created a space that was stunning to look at when guests entered the home but was still casual and functional for her teenagers.

The formal round glass tables were moved upstairs to her bedroom where they worked beautifully. In the 'hangout' we used some wooden chests we found that were more functional. They could be used as tables for drinks or food and also provided great storage for video games and other items.

When we were done, the room looked incredible and her teenagers loved it. It was functional and gave them the cozy, cave-like feeling they wanted. We had achieved our objective of combining functionality and appearance.

Her son came home at the end of the day and instantly began to use the room. This, our client said, was the biggest compliment he could have paid us.

BEFORE: *This was the first room you saw when you came in the front door. The homeowner wanted it to be the family room because the room beyond had a fireplace and made a cozier living room. However, since this space was visible by everyone entering the home we needed to make it attractive as well as functional. Conflicting colors in the artwork and rug also made the room feel 'busy.'*

AFTER: *To create better color harmony in the room we brought in the homeowner's dark grey artwork, which worked beautifully with the soft grey furniture. We then switched the brightly colored carpet for one with taupe and grey colors. The angle of the furniture also draws your eye, and the traffic flow, to the room beyond. This room is now functional for teenagers and still looks great.*

That's it for Step 1 of redesigning your home. The following questionnaire will help you complete this step.

A FORM FOR ASSESSING *YOUR* NEEDS

Below is a questionnaire to get you started analyzing your home and your needs. Feel free to ask yourself other questions as well. Also, ask the other members of your family what they think. You want everyone in the home to love it when you're done.

You will need to ask yourself many of these questions in every room of your home. I recommend starting with the public rooms first and working your way to the more private rooms in the following order: living room, family room, dining room, master bedroom, kitchen, children's bedrooms, guest room, den/office, other.

When you actually do the redesign, you may want to do the living room and family room at the same time if they contain furniture and art that can be switched between rooms. If not, they can be done separately. In some homes, it's nice to do the living room and dining room at the same time. Choose whichever format makes the most sense for you.

QUESTIONNAIRE

1. What pictures do you love the most in your home? Which ones do you want highlighted?

_____

_____

_____

2. What items of furniture do you love the most? Which are the most comfortable? The most attractive to you?

_____

_____

_____

3. What accessories are special to you? What accessories make you cringe when you look at them?

_____

_____

_____

4. What mood would you like your room to have?

_____

_____

5. How do you use the room now and how could the space be better utilized?

_____

_____

_____

6. How do you entertain? How many people sit in the living room and chat? How many sit around the dining room table? How many people watch TV at any one time? Do you need more than one conversation area in the living room? For small spaces, can you create a "quick change" room so it can do double or triple duty?

_____

_____

_____

_____

7. How many places do you have where someone can curl up with a book? _____ Is it adequate? _____ Do you even use it? _____

8. How many people live in the home? What are their needs? (a place to do homework, a home office, etc.)

_____

_____

_____

9. Are there any other special considerations you need to take into account? (pets, people with physical challenges, hobbies, etc.)

_____

_____

_____

10. Are there any restrictions or limitations like a piano that needs an inside wall or must go in a certain room, or a TV and stereo that are wired together so that they need to stay together?

_____

_____

11. Are there any plants that need a certain spot for light?

_____

_____

12. Are there certain chairs that someone must use to watch TV?

_____

_____

_____

13. Are there pictures and pieces of furniture in the basement, garage, or closets that you may want to bring out in the open again (or give away or sell?)

_____

_____

_____

_____

14. Add here anything else you need to know about your home and the people who live there before you get started.

_____

_____

_____

_____

_____

_____

_____

_____

_____

_____

_____

_____

_____

The Art of Redesign

STEP 2 | Space

Before you can begin to redesign a space, it must be cleared. That means taking all the furniture, art, and accessories out of a room so you can start from scratch. Clearing the room gives you a clean-slate perspective so you have all possible options available to you.

Let's talk a bit about how we tend to do our rooms now. Some people decide they don't like their furniture arrangement, so they move the furniture around. However, their art is still in the same place on the walls. Whether you know it or not, where your art is hung will affect your furniture placement options.

Other people keep buying new accessories thinking it will make their room feel "right." I see this all the time. What you need to realize, though, is that if the furniture isn't placed properly, and the art isn't hung properly, you can accessorize all you want but it won't make the room work.

Designing your room is like putting together an outfit. If your pants and skirt don't work together, adding a jacket and shoes will just make it worse because now nothing works together. Adding jewelry won't make the outfit work either. And if you add more and more jewelry you just look worse.

It's the same way with your furniture. Your furniture has to be placed properly, and then you hang the art to work with the furniture. At that point, you really don't even need accessories; the room will already feel fabulous. Then, a few well-placed accessories will bring out your personality and add that final touch to the room.

Saying all this leads me to the most important thing you can do in redesigning your room: Take everything out of the room first.

As I mentioned, you need to take all the accessories out of the room and all the art off the walls. Ideally you would also remove all the furniture. However, for practical reasons you can leave the large pieces of furniture in the room – bookcases, pianos, sofa and main seating chairs. These need to be placed first anyway. I'll discuss this in more detail later. Removing things from the room gives you the clean-slate perspective of the room necessary to do the redesign. Let me give you an example where I didn't follow my own advice.

 STORIES
from Redesign

I remember doing a couple's living room. My assistant and I had taken the art off the walls and removed everything else. However, there was a stereo cabinet beside the fireplace. We knew it was wrong where it was because of the huge weight of both pieces side by side. But it looked heavy and we didn't want to move it. "Let's just place the rest of the furniture first, and then move the cabinet," I heard myself say. So we tried to make a conversation grouping with the chairs and sofa. We tried some options. Nothing worked. We tried more options. Nothing worked. We struggled more and got really creative. Nothing worked. Finally I said, "Okay, this isn't working. Let's take a break and move the stereo cabinet because we know it's in the wrong place." We moved it to where it belonged, and then went back to making a conversation grouping. In five minutes we had a fabulous conversation grouping that worked beautifully.

I give you this example so you realize how things in the room affect your eye, even when you try to pretend they're not there. You really need to take everything out of the room and start over.

STEPS FOR DISMANTLING THE ROOM

✷ Remove everything but the large pieces of furniture from the room. If possible, arrange those so that they look 'wrong' in the room. This is so that your eye doesn't assume that the space it occupies is permanent. I usually leave the sofa/loveseat, whatever chairs I know I want in my conversation area, big armoires, entertainment units, and pianos, in the room. Everything else goes out.

✷ Remove the pictures and place them in another room such as a bedroom, lining them around the walls or laying them out on the bed so you can see them.

✷ Put pictures with like characteristics together, forming pairs and collections, to help you with groupings later.

✷ Decide upon a "staging" area — maybe the dining room table or kitchen counter — and put all accessories, such as figurines, books, and photos there. Small plants are considered accessories and should go in the staging area. Start putting things into like groups as you set them on the staging area to help you form collections later. For example, brass with brass, crystal with crystal, red with red, teapots with teapots, and candles with other candles. This also saves time when accessorizing the room and helps you identify color, themes, and personality threads.

✷ Put lamps, large plants, area rugs, and small tables in another room. (Large plants and area rugs are considered furniture for the purposes of redesign).

Note: When taking things off shelves, always take things off from the bottom up and replace from the top down to avoid breakage of items underneath, should you drop an item or the shelf slips or breaks. (The exception is bookcases that are not attached to the wall. In that case you take things off from the top down and replace from the bottom up so the bookcase doesn't tip.)

ARCHITECTURAL LINES

Now that you have dismantled the room it's easier to look around and see what you have to work with. Where are the architectural lines in the room? Are there walls that end, creating an invisible wall across the room and effectively making it two rooms? Where are the doorways, windows, little alcoves? How high are the windowsills? What is the shape of the room? The shape of the ceiling? Are there beams in the ceiling? What about pitched ceilings or alcoves? Where are the highs and lows? Make sure you are aware of all the little intricacies in the room. You will want to work with them as much as possible during your redesign.

BEFORE: *The sofa in this room cut off the pretty window, making the room feel small.*

The Art of Redesign

AFTER: *Look at the difference in space and how pretty the window looks now. Basically, we just flipped the sofa and the two chairs. It's always better if you can walk up to a window. It creates a sense of space and beauty in a room.*

THE FIVE ROOM SHAPES ARE:

✸ Square

✸ Rectangle

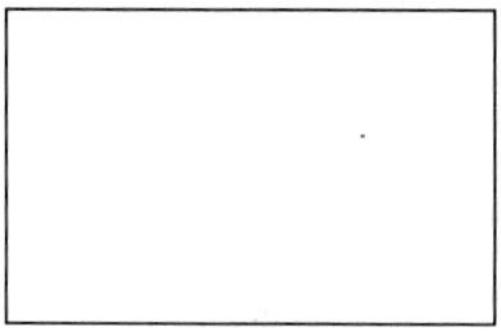

✸ Oblong (or bowling alley)

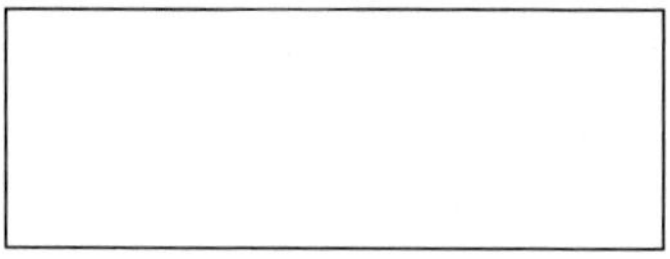

✸ L-shaped

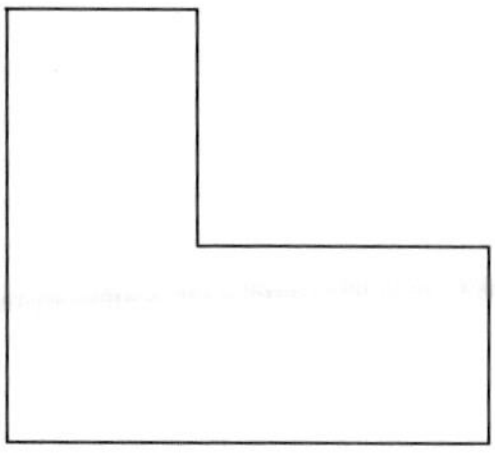

✸ Odd-angled

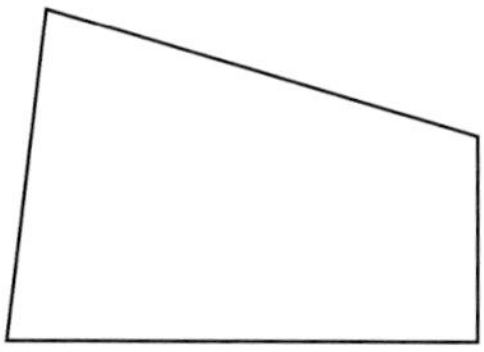

BEFORE: *The wall on the right of this foyer had a beautiful curve in it. This is an architectural feature that you want to highlight and work with. The rectangular table is fighting with the architectural lines of the home.*

AFTER: *By putting a rectangular piece on the rectangular wall, and a piece with curves that fits into the curve of the other wall, we are working with the home's architectural lines. Now the beautiful curve in the wall is emphasized.*

THE FIVE CEILING SHAPES ARE:

* ❋ Flat
* ❋ Cathedral (dome)
* ❋ Pitched (or vaulted)
* ❋ Step-Up
* ❋ Any of the above in combination

Nothing should be placed without regard to the lines of the article and the lines (especially architectural lines) around it. The bigger the article, the more important it is to follow this rule. For example, any large piece of furniture in front of the window or in front of a large wall needs to be centered on that wall or window or lined up with the end of the wall or window and balanced with something else on the other side. This creates an imperceptible sense of balance and harmony in the room. If placed in front of a window, furniture should always fit below the windowsill. Otherwise it creates too many horizontal lines and will appear 'busy.'

CHOOSING THE PRIMARY FOCAL POINT

Now it's time for the big decision. What will be your primary focal point? As much as possible, you will want your primary focal point to be a natural/architectural feature of the room. If you have a huge fireplace it's pretty hard to not have it be the primary focal point of the room. You would have to create something outstanding enough and visually heavy enough to take the focus away from the fireplace. This is a challenge that most of us wouldn't choose. So if you have a fireplace in the room, then that will normally be your primary focal point. A window with a gorgeous view of the ocean, mountains, or garden is another possibility for a primary focal point. The difficulty here is that at night it just may become a big, black hole. So often it's better to create a different primary focal point and incorporate the view as a secondary focal point in the room.

Televisions are often chosen as primary focal points in a room. I try everything I can to create a different primary focal point, and then incorporate the TV as a secondary focal point. If there's a large entertainment center, however, then the entertainment center may have to be the primary focal point just because of its size and weight.

If there isn't an obvious natural/architectural focal point in the room, then you will need to create a primary focal point. There are numerous ways you can do this.

In one home we created a primary focal point using a small table surrounded by two chairs with art over the table and coordinating accessories on the table. It was gorgeous! In another home we used a large armoire. In another we used a beautiful Japanese screen with a chair beside it. A beautiful piano can be a focal point, or any other beautiful large piece of furniture. A huge painting that's visually heavy can be a primary focal point. If it's over a table or has plants around or under it, that will enhance it even more. Speaking of plants, a collection of tall, medium, and small plants can make a stunning primary focal point in the room. Put some art with it and/or a chair beside it to increase its visual weight and interest.

BEFORE: *The front door of the home was to the right of this photo. When you walked into the room, the large TV dominated the space. The fireplace, which should have been the primary focal point in the room, was eclipsed by the TV. There also wasn't a cozy conversation area in the room. The furniture was lined up for TV viewing.*

AFTER: *By moving the TV to the left of the fireplace we were able to make the fireplace the primary focal point in the room. We also increased the seating in the room and created a nice conversation area that faced the primary focal point (the fireplace) as well as the TV.*

BEFORE: *This living room didn't have a primary focal point, making the room feel disjointed. The sofa should never be part of the primary focal point. It must face or 'address' the primary focal point.*

BEFORE: *The TV cabinet was dominating the room and was cluttered with too many things. There was so much going on between the art and the accessories that focusing on any particular element was almost impossible.*

43

BEFORE: *When you entered the room the furniture blocked the entry to the room, making it uninviting.*

AFTER: *We created a primary focal point using a large piece of art flanked by two smaller pieces, placing the TV to the left of the primary focal point.*

AFTER: *We moved the sofa to face the primary focal point in the room. Angling the sofa also made the room more inviting.*

AFTER: *Splitting up the TV cabinet allowed us to have a piece at the front door to create a foyer effect without blocking the entrance to the room. Adding a patterned fabric to the chairs helped balance the visual weight of the dark sofa.*

COMMON FOCAL POINTS

❋ Living room or family room – usually the fireplace or
large window with a view is the primary focal point. As I
mentioned, you can also create a focal point with an armoire,
an entertainment center, or a chest with artwork above it.
In the living room or family room there may be more than
one focal point. However, you will need to choose a primary
focal point because it anchors the main conversation-seating
grouping. Secondary focal points can be a nice view out the
window, a TV, etc. It is nice to incorporate these as part of the
conversation area, even though they are not the 'primary'
focal point.

BEFORE: *This little sitting
room off the kitchen needed
a focal point and a nice
conversation area.*

AFTER: *By bringing in a large red armoire, we added color and a primary focal point to the
room. The clown hanging from the ceiling and the little horse on the wall added some fun to
the design and reflected the personality of the homeowners.*

✳ Dining room – a buffet or sideboard with a large painting, a grouping, or a framed mirror above it, an extremely large oil painting by itself, a wall of sliding or French doors, or a large picture window, are all potential primary focal points.

BEFORE: *This dining room had conflicting focal points without one standing out as the primary. The "main event" should be obvious so your eye knows where to land in the room.*

AFTER: *Putting brightly colored art in the alcove over a brightly colored table created the emphasis we needed in this room. Now there is no doubt about where the primary focal point is. We moved the light-colored cabinet to the kitchen where it worked perfectly.*

✳ Bedroom – the bed is the primary focal point. Have a fancy headboard or hang pictures over the bed, and flank the bed with tables and lamps to make it more important. Occasionally a wall of glass doors or windows that reveal a great view may be the focal point of the bedroom. However you need to think about what it looks like at night. Often it's just a wall of drapes.

Once you choose a primary focal point, you want to reinforce it by placing other furnishings and accessories to balance and emphasize it. For example, in the living room your conversation area should face the primary focal point. If you have an L-shaped living/dining room, each area needs its own focal point.

I can't emphasize how important it is to create a conversation area facing the primary focal point. I have been in homes where the conversation area was positioned with its back to the fireplace, facing a television. The whole room just felt wrong and my impulse was to flee immediately rather than stay and relax in the room. You can't ignore something as large as a fireplace in the room. Even if you don't like it, work with it. By using art and accessories that complement the fireplace you can start to appreciate beauty in it that you may not have noticed before.

STORIES
from Redesign

> I remember redesigning a home where the homeowner told me during the consultation that they were going to tear out the fireplace because they didn't like it. After we finished the redesign, one of her first comments to me was, "We don't even have to replace the fireplace any more!"
>
> Another client thought she needed built-in cabinets on either side of her fireplace because she could never make it work with the lovely character windows on either side. Her comment to us when we were done? "Now I don't have to get built-in cabinets!"

Time and time again I have discovered that if every item is complementing each other item in the room, things that previously looked ugly and were going to be replaced, now look beautiful.

CLUTTER

I know you've been hearing about de-cluttering ad nauseum. It's on TV, in all the decorating magazines, and it's getting kind of tiring. However, it's critically important. Getting rid of clutter will change your life.

Think about it. When you walk into a cluttered room or look in that cluttered closet, your heart drops. Imperceptibly, bit by bit, you are dealing with negativity in your own home. Isn't there enough of that out in the world? You just don't need those kinds of feelings in your home. Your home needs to be a place of refuge; a place that makes you smile when you look around. It's clean, it's harmonious, it flows, and you feel good when you're in the rooms. If there are any places in your home that make your heart sink, you need to tackle them — right away.

Think about how you feel when your office desk is cluttered. It's hard to concentrate. Your thoughts are scattered and you jump from one thing to another. That's how clutter in your home impacts you. Getting rid of it will help you focus. You will also feel more calm and relaxed. Think of the energy that can generate!

Let's define clutter. Clutter isn't just having a lot of things. If you have a lot of possessions that you love, or that are useful, and they all have a place where they are stored or displayed, then it's not clutter.

Clutter is being surrounded by things you don't love or don't need. Look at each item you own and ask yourself two questions:

1. Do I love it? If yes, keep it. If no, go on to question two.

2. Do I need it? If you used it in the last year or definitely plan to use it in the next six months, it can stay. If not, it needs to go.

What about those of you who love everything? You're so sentimental that you can't throw away the art your daughter did in grades 3, 4, 5 ... even though she's married with three children of her own now. Find a loving friend or a trained professional organizer to help you let go. At this point, you don't own it, it owns you.

What if you think you'll need it someday? Get rid of it. Chances are you'll forget you have it by the time you really do need it and you'll buy a new one anyway. Or it won't work anymore, or you won't be able to find it because you have so much stuff.

BEFORE: *This gorgeous sunroom off the living room had turned into a catch-all for clutter.*

AFTER: *Now it's a beautiful room in which to play a piano.*

Some of us have parents who were affected by the Depression or they didn't have a lot of money, and we were brought up never to throw anything away. This kind of conditioning makes it difficult for us to part with things. It's important to really look at why you're keeping them and whether it makes sense for you now. I will never need 100 elastic bands or 200 twist ties or 300 plastic grocery bags. It's okay for me to get rid of most of them and just keep a few that I will need. They are easy to acquire if I ever need more.

Maybe you love reading and can't stand to get rid of a book, newspaper, or magazine. Ask yourself if you'll ever read it again. Honestly. If yes, then keep it. If no, please give it to those who don't have access to books. Give your magazines to professionals you know who have a waiting room — doctors, dentists, hair stylists, hospitals.

BEFORE: *The piano we put in the sunroom had previously been in the dining room, making the room crowded.*

AFTER: *With the piano gone, they now have a gorgeous dining room. The homeowner had been thinking of buying new dining room furniture but after the redesign, fell in love with the old one all over again.*

For most women, clothes are an issue. We always think we'll wear them again one day. Or that the style will come back. I've caught myself saying "But it's a good wool suit. It's a classic. I know I'll wear it one day." I kept my suits for ten years based on that premise. The reality is that if I did need a suit, I didn't want to wear 'that old thing' and I bought a new one anyway. So I finally gave them all away and have never missed them. I also have the satisfaction of knowing that perhaps someone out there is using them and loving them. I now go through my closet every six months and give things away. It makes it easy for me if I imagine someone with no money standing in front of me lovingly looking at the item in my hand. Would I give it to them? If the answer is yes, it goes in the donation bag. Also, whenever I buy anything new I try to give away one or two items so that the overall number doesn't increase. This works for everything in your home — not just clothing.

Finally, there are those items that are expensive. It's hard to sell or give away items that we know cost a lot. However, if we don't love them or need them, it's better to give them to someone who does. This not only helps someone else, but frees up space in our lives for new things that we do love or can use.

AFTER: *This antique sewing machine had been "stored" in the sunroom. Now it's creating a beautiful vignette in the living room.*

FENG SHUI

The basic principles of feng shui are balance, harmony, flow, and being surrounded by things you love. This makes sense to me. Redesign is based on those same principles, so effectively we are doing 'intuitive feng shui' when we redesign our homes. I am not a feng shui expert and I don't pay attention to the bagua, the wealth corner, etc. However, some of the feng shui principles just make good sense to me, so I've adopted those.

There's a feng shui principle that says you need to get rid of the old to make room for new things to come into your life. I was at a seminar one day listening to a feng shui expert talk about her experiences. She had come from a scientific background. (It always amazed me that she even became a feng shui expert given her background). Anyway, she would try things just to see if she could get some kind of proof. Based on the above principle, she got rid of all her clothes from her past (scientific) life. She didn't have the money to buy new ones so just waited for the 'new' to come into her life. A few days later she was invited to visit a friend in California for a couple of weeks. She went there with two T-shirts and a pair of jeans — the only clothes that she had kept. After a week, her friend got tired of seeing her in the same clothes every day. "Here," she said, handing her two boxes full of clothes. "I was going to give these away but it just occurred to me that they might fit you." She opened the boxes and there were all the types of clothes that totally fit her new lifestyle. She now has a closet full of clothes that work for her instead of a closet full of clothes that don't. It's hard to argue with results like that.

START WITH YOUR NEW, REDESIGNED PLACE IN MIND

This will help you organize items into your three useful categories: keep, sell/donate, and throw away.

As you handle each item in your home, from old clothing to tabletop collections, ask yourself if you can picture that item in your 'new' home. Is there a place for it? Isn't this a perfect excuse to get rid of Aunt Hilda's cross-stitch sampler?

Start with your least favorite or messiest room. Make a list that you can go through systematically, with categories such as tabletops, closets, and under the bed. That way each one can be checked off with a satisfying flourish as you make progress.

Clear all tabletops first, using your keep, sell/donate, or throw-away rule. Next, clean out the closets, and so on. Throw away as you go along by actually taking bags of trash to the dumpster. That way you won't be tempted to keep things that should be ditched.

I know, I know, those crystal decanters your great aunt left you are very expensive. But if you don't love them, they'll only make you feel bad every time you look at them. Why keep something in your home that doesn't give you joy? Much better to let someone else love them. You can buy something you'll love instead.

FOLLOW THE ONE-YEAR RULE

It's hard to predict what you are going to need, but it's very safe to assume that if you haven't worn an article of clothing, or read that paperback in a year, that it's pretty safe to sell it, give it away, or throw it out.

YOU DON'T NEED TO DISPLAY EVERYTHING YOU OWN ALL AT ONCE

Sometimes even after you get rid of all the clutter, you just have too many possessions. The home will look cluttered if you use them all. In that case, you need to make some decisions about what is used in the redesign and what is 'left over.' Many of the items that you don't use can be saved and swapped with something at a later date. Perhaps you use a number of collections or items during the summer and then swap them for other items or collections in the winter months. Or perhaps you just wait till you get tired of seeing certain things. At that time you can give yourself a fresh new look with the items you stored away. You can do the same thing with your art if you have too much art to display all at once.

NOW CLEAR THE SPACE

This step is imperative before moving on. I know it seems like a lot of work, but take heart. It can be done. And it goes faster than you would think. Let me give you an example of why this step is so important.

STORIES
from Redesign

Valerie was a client of mine who had gone through a difficult divorce and was now ready for change. When I met Valerie at her front door I thought, 'what an open, friendly, lovely person.'

But when I walked into her dining room/living room I couldn't believe it! I could hardly breathe. There was so ... much ... stuff! It was overwhelming. I looked at Valerie and looked at these rooms and could not equate the two at all. There was a huge disconnect between the lively, open woman standing in front of me and the closed, stifling rooms.

"I'd like to have a more minimalist, Asian-feeling room," Valerie said, "but I can't afford to buy anything new and don't know where to start."

I was a little concerned that taking this tired, old-looking, cluttered home and making it peaceful-Asian might be more of a challenge than I could meet. But I remembered the other times magic had happened when I redesigned a home. So I leapt right in and started asking her questions about the different pieces in her home.

The dining room was a mish-mash of different furniture colors and styles: a dark corner china cabinet, a teak table too big for the space, and an oak roll-top desk. A huge pile of accessories rested on top of the china cabinet, and a huge fountain resided on the floor between the living room and dining room. The speakers for the stereo were the size of end tables. I hopefully asked if the table could be made smaller.

"No," was the answer I didn't want to hear.

I then asked if she used the roll-top desk, hoping maybe we could move it to the basement. Unfortunately she really wanted it to stay. She also loved the fountain. Thankfully, though, she agreed to get smaller speakers. I asked her some questions about the art in the dining room and noticed a gorgeous Oriental doll buried in all the stuff on top of the china cabinet. I also spotted some lovely art pieces with an Oriental flavor hiding in the hallway.

Then we moved further into the living room. A huge particleboard entertainment unit towered over the room, dominating a whole wall.

"That piece makes the room feel small," I said. "It would be better if we could take out the TV and stereo and put them on top of a beautiful low piece, maybe one with an Asian feel."

I then looked around at the mismatched oak tables, the old sofa and chair, and once again felt that giving her what she wanted was impossible. Distracting myself, I asked her about the art and different accessories in the room. Some of the pieces were sentimental and had interesting stories, like the painting her son had done for her. Others she didn't really care about. They'd just accumulated over time.

"Okay, Valerie," I said. "You realize that we're going to have a lot of things left over if we're to give you the home you want. Where can I put them?"

"Just leave it all in a pile by the back door downstairs and I'll deal with it," she said.

We then toured the rest of her home, talking specifically about the clutter in her bedroom: which pieces had sentimental value, which pieces she loved, and which pieces she could now let go.

We set a date for the redesign and I left. On the way home I turned over all the challenges the home presented: small rooms, lots of old, dated items, and Valerie's desire to have an Asian-inspired home.

"Well," I thought, "I can only do my best and we'll see what happens."

During the week Valerie called to say she'd found two small speakers on sale and a second-hand chest in a consignment store. She had put the chest on hold till I could go see if it would work. Her friend had also told her to buy another large cabinet, and she wanted me to decide.

When I went to the store the decision was easy. The friend's suggestion was another cheap particleboard piece that definitely wouldn't work. Then, I spotted a gorgeous low piece with spare detailing that matched the Oriental flavor Valerie wanted: her name was on it and there was a price tag of only $40!

The day of the redesign finally arrived. I was teaching a course and Valerie's home was one of our hands-on learning opportunities. My students were appalled when they walked into Valerie's home.

"How can we possibly make this look good?" they asked.

"No problem," I bluffed. "We'll just follow the system and magic will happen." As I looked at their faces, the disbelief was evident and matched the way I was feeling inside. Fortunately I'd done enough homes to know that I'd felt this way before and it had always turned out wonderfully.

So I rallied the troops, and we started following the system I'll be outlining in this book. Over the course of the day the transformation gradually occurred. At the end of the day we were shocked. Valerie's home was calm, serene, open, spacious, warm, inviting and, most remarkably, had an Asian feel to it.

BEFORE: *The huge cabinet in this living room not only blocked light from the window but was a refuge for clutter.*

AFTER: *Look at the difference it makes to get rid of all that stuff. The light in the room is increased and the function is improved. Which room would you rather live in?*

Instead of wanting to turn around and run from the space, we felt ourselves lingering and just enjoying the feeling of being in this lovely, harmonious place.

We were a little nervous, though. There was a pile of unused 'stuff' four feet high by five feet wide downstairs by her back door. Would she be okay with that?

Valerie walked in, and we anxiously waited for her reaction. A look of total disbelief and shock came over her face. Then tears welled up in her eyes.

"It's so beautiful," she whispered. "I can't believe this is my home — and you made it look this way using my own things." As she looked around the space, taking it all in, she repeated over and over, "Oh my god, I love it."

My students' eyes filled with tears as Valerie and I hugged each other.

"I can't thank you enough," she said. "I've been changing a lot of things in my life and now you've given me the home I needed to move to the next phase. Thank you, thank you, thank you."

My class and I were on a natural high when we left Valerie's home. We'd worked hard and created a beautiful, warm home for Valerie to enjoy and proudly show her friends.

One of my students said, "I really thought you were crazy when you said she wanted an Asian-feeling home out of that. But we did it. And we used her existing furnishings."

Months later Valerie told me that she made changes in other aspects of her life, inspired by her new living space. She was changing some of her personal relationships that weren't working for her. What could be a better gift for someone than that?

AFTER: *The large cabinet wasn't wasted either. The scale of it worked perfectly in the basement where we created a TV room for the homeowner's boarders.*

BEFORE: *The balance was off in the dining room because the corner cabinet was on the brick wall which is visually heavy. Anything with a pattern has higher visual weight than something solid. Also, the mirror just reflected clutter on the other side of the room so didn't give you anything attractive to look at.*

AFTER: *Moving the cabinet to the other side, including a lamp to highlight the brick, and replacing the mirror with a nice piece of art made the room feel balanced and peaceful.*

STEP 3 | Big Stuff

Finally, we can move into reincorporating furnishings into the room. For this and the remainder of the steps, you will need the assistance of a good friend. I recommend choosing one who loves to laugh, is creative, and will tell you exactly what he or she thinks. This person will not only help you with the physical aspects of your redesign, but will help you with objectivity and creativity.

The most difficult thing in redesigning your own home can be a lack of objectivity. We don't always have objectivity when the home is ours. We have emotional relationships with things, and hence can't think creatively as well as someone who is objective. Your friend can bring a fresh new perspective to the process.

Your friend can also help you with the creative process. Let me illustrate the impact of having someone to share your creative ideas with. If I think of an idea, then it may be good or bad, but it's just that: an idea. If, however, I have someone to share my creativity with, then that person can build on my idea or take it in a new direction that I hadn't thought of. Then I can build on that, and then they can build on it again, and so on. We can end up somewhere amazing, instead of stopping at my initial idea.

So find that perfect friend to help you. Perhaps you can then help her redesign her home so you both benefit.

It is also critically important that you follow the steps in order. Once the room is dismantled (Step Two), you place the furniture first (Step Three), then the wall art (Step Four), and then the accessories (Step Five). Do not start accessorizing before placing the wall art. Also, do not try to leave the art in the room and rearrange the furniture. Whether you realize it or not, the art will be dictating furniture patterns. The key to an amazing redesign of your home is to follow the steps in the exact order presented. Let me give you an example of furniture that was out of place and in the wrong room, to highlight the impact furniture placement has on a home.

STORIES
from Redesign

It had been two years since Sarah had moved in with Greg into what had been his family home with his previous wife. He was a collector of art and accessories – and they were everywhere. Sarah had brought some of her own things into the home but the result was just more clutter. Her beautiful sofa was in the bedroom, cluttering up the room. Her tall étagère was in a corner of the living room with a number of her beautiful glass, china and oriental things artfully arranged. However it looked out of place with Greg's heavy brown leather furniture and his oil landscapes.

In the family room, the clean-lined black leather furniture wasn't working with the dark brown wood paneling of the room and Greg's mom's gorgeous oak buffet looked sad and out of place. My first reaction was that all the paneling would have to be painted cream or white in order for it to work. Over the mantel, Sarah had hung her oil painting of stylized horses that had warm oranges, golds and reds in it. Unfortunately this just made the stark black furniture in the room look more out of place.

The dining room had a huge white table, a large white china cabinet, and another huge white cabinet that took up the whole length of the room pretty much from floor to ceiling. The effect was stifling. There was hardly room to get into your chair at the dining room table.

After a lengthy consultation with Sarah and Greg, we decided that the huge white cabinet in the dining room could be moved to the basement where it could store a lot of the things that they didn't use on a frequent basis. We also decided to put the black leather furniture from the family room into the basement and move the gorgeous brown leather furniture into the family room. This left space for Sarah's beautiful sofa and armchair to go into the living room, freeing up space in the bedroom. Both Sarah and Greg were concerned that there wouldn't be enough seating in the living room but I told them not to worry, we would figure it out. We agreed that they would have these items moved prior to the day of the redesign.

I also made a list of all the accessories that were important to them. The rest would go downstairs in the storage cabinet.

When I walked into their home to do the redesign, it was already better. Sarah's cream and tan brocade sofa worked beautifully with the étagère and the soft cream draperies in the room. We brought in Greg's Japanese screen that we found tucked in the corner between the wall and china cabinet in the dining room and made it a focal point in the left-hand corner as you walked into the room. We moved the buffet from the family room into the living room to balance the weight of the étagère on the other side of the room. The matching brocade armchair from the bedroom and two cream-and-tan Parsons Chairs from Sarah's old dining room suite completed the conversation area. A black oriental chair and a black antique chair placed by the screen made a secondary 'nook' and provided extra seating that could easily be pulled into the conversation area. The heavy blue and green landscapes were all taken out of the room and replaced with light, airy paintings that worked with the rest of the furnishings. Accessories that belonged to both Sarah and Greg were artfully arranged in the room. The result was a stunning formal living room that looked like every piece had been purchased specifically for that room. The angled furniture arrangement made the formal room feel warm and inviting. Strategically placed lamps invited you to sit down with a book or have a glass of wine.

In the family room, the rich brown leather furniture worked so beautifully with the wooden wall paneling that we no longer felt the need to paint it. Removing the buffet gave us wall space to hang a huge painting that Greg loved. It had been hung in an upstairs hallway since there wasn't a wall big enough for it downstairs. Now everyone could appreciate it. Sarah's stylized horses over the mantel now picked up the warm tones in the furniture. A few more pieces of art that Greg loved, and some plants and accessories that they both loved, completed the warm, cozy room.

Now for the dining room. With the huge cabinet gone, we were able to hang a collection of the gorgeous landscapes in the dining room. The walls in the dining room had been painted a deep green and the rich green-and-blue landscapes, which had looked out of place in the cream-colored living room, now came alive. All the extraneous items were taken downstairs and only the pieces that Greg and Sarah loved were displayed in the china cabinet. The result was quite effective.

When Greg and Sarah came home, they were stunned. Greg kept saying he had been trying to imagine what we would do in the rooms, or how we would handle all the art that they had both collected. He was particularly excited about the painting in the family room.

I was eager to show them how we had highlighted everything they both loved so that the home now incorporated both of them in a cohesive way. It felt like we had taken a disjointed relationship and brought it together. I was surprised by how relatively quiet Sarah was, having expected her to show some excitement.

After touring them through the rooms and pointing out everything we had done, Sarah and I returned to the living room for another look. With tears in her eyes, Sarah said, "In two years, this is the first time I've felt like this was my home. Thank you."

CREATIVITY

Before we get started on placing the furniture (Big Stuff) to create balance and harmony in a room, I want to talk a bit about creativity. If you are struggling with the placement of something, or feeling frustrated or in a rush, creativity goes out the window. Imagine the difference if you're feeling joyful, playful, and child-like. What possibilities are now open to you? Would you ever think of using that old wrought-iron gate from your garden as a focal piece on the dining room wall if you weren't feeling playful? That's where creativity lies — in the joyful 'try anything' side of you.

So pay attention to your frame of mind when redesigning your home. Adopt that child-like, playful attitude. This is not serious business. It's play! If you find yourself struggling with something and it feels hard, then stop and do something else for a while until you're feeling playful again. Then come back to it. You need to be feeling playful in order to be creative.

Here are some tricks you can try to get yourself back into a playful mood if things start to become a struggle.

* ✳ Look in a mirror and make funny faces at yourself.
* ✳ Go for a walk around the block.
* ✳ Turn on your favorite music and dance around the room.
* ✳ Go play in another room for a while
* ✳ Start trying truly crazy ideas that you know won't work (sometimes you get fabulous surprises when you do this.)

Okay, now that we've got the right frame of mind, we can get started. We will begin with living rooms and family rooms, as these are the highest public-impact rooms.

PLACE THE LARGEST PIECES OF FURNITURE FIRST

You want to place the largest pieces of furniture, such as an armoire or a piano, first because normally there are only one or two spots in the room where they will fit. Also, they must be placed to balance the room. If you have a large fireplace in the room, then you need to use your largest piece of furniture to balance the weight of it on the other side of the room. Therefore the first place to put your large armoire or piano would be directly across from the fireplace (or your primary focal point). If that's not possible, then try to place it in one of the corners diagonally across from the fireplace. And if that's not possible, then place it in the center of one of the walls perpendicular to the fireplace. Basically, the farther away from the fireplace the large piece is, the easier it will be to balance the room.

BEFORE: *The weight of the bookcase and the piano next to the fireplace caused an imbalance in the room and made the room feel crowded. Also, the piano was scrunched into a corner, making the room feel small. It also wasn't working with the architectural lines of the staircase.*

AFTER: *We moved the bookcase to the other side of the room across from a second bookcase. Then we angled the piano so that there was space around it. It now works with the lines of the staircase better as well. The view toward the fireplace and piano is now spacious and clean.*

The highest piece of furniture should generally be under the highest point in the ceiling. If there is a beamed ceiling, any tall piece will probably need to be centered on one of the beams or placed on one side and balanced with something else on the other.

BEFORE: *The sofa was placed across the window pointed at the entrance to the room. It's quite common to put the sofa against the longest wall. However, that just emphasizes the length of the wall. Try to find a way to angle the sofa or put it against a shorter wall.*

AFTER: *By angling the sofa, the conversation area now takes in the view out the windows as well as the fireplace. The bookcase was angled to mirror the angle of the piano across from it. Diagonal lines and triangles are always more pleasing than anything "straight on." The result is a cozy conversation area and a more balanced, spacious feeling in the room.*

PIANOS

Always hire professionals to move a piano — it's a delicate instrument. Also, remember that when you move a piano it usually needs to be re-tuned afterward.

As a piano is usually the largest piece of furniture in a room, its placement should be decided before anything else.

First let's look at which room it should be in. The most common options for pianos are the living room, dining room, or family room. Occasionally you may have a den or a sunroom that works as well. Look for a space that the pianist in the home would like to be in. Also, keep the piano in a separate room from the television so that someone can still play it while someone else is watching TV.

Since pianos are so large, they will affect the balance in the room quite dramatically. If you have a fireplace in the room, the natural place for the piano would be across from, not next to, the fireplace. This placement balances the weight of the two pieces. In a smaller room, a piano angled in a corner can balance a sofa, loveseat, or other weighty piece angled in the corner diagonally across from it.

Just as with any large piece of furniture, there should be at least a foot of wall space on both sides of a piano. Never shove it into a corner. If you lack space, angling the piano into the corner will help. If your piano is particularly attractive, and you don't have a natural or architectural focal point in the room, then you can use the piano as the focal point.

BEFORE: *These young newlyweds had all new furniture but didn't know where to put it. They were musicians and wanted a large area for jam sessions. So they turned the living room into a dining room, thinking they'd have more space in the back of the house. What they didn't realize was that the architecture dictated that it was two small rooms, not one large room (because of the dropped ceiling between the two spaces).*

AFTER: *From one dysfunctional space to two functional spaces. We turned the two spaces into a TV room for the couple and a dining room. On the right-hand side of the dining room were patio doors onto a deck.*

BEFORE: *This is a photo of the original living room turned into a dining room. The front door is in the top right-hand corner just out of the photo. The homeowner didn't like that you walked right into the room off the street. She wanted to create a foyer but wasn't sure how.*

AFTER: *Now with this transformed living room they have the huge space they wanted for their jam sessions. The pianist was particularly pleased because she now looked into the room instead of into a wall. There was even space to bring in more seating. By strategically placing the bookcase we created a foyer without visually closing off the space. This young couple now had everything they wanted.*

Many people feel they have to place a piano on an inside wall. The reason for this is that an outside wall can affect the humidity, and thus the wood of the piano. In addition, the sound reverberating from an outside wall is different than from an inside wall. However, most modern homes are better insulated than in the past so the humidity problem isn't a concern. Also, if your piano isn't ever used by a concert pianist, you won't notice the difference in sound. In both these situations, an outside wall for the piano is fine.

If you have a grand piano, it should be placed with the harp pointing into the room so that the pianist will face the room. If possible, the curved part of the harp should be visible from the entrance. The most dramatic placement is the diagonal. If the room is large enough, angle it from a corner. You want to enjoy the curve of the piano.

DEALING WITH THE TV, STEREO AND OTHER ELECTRONICS

One of the most difficult pieces to place is the television. Your ideal is to have the television be a secondary, not the primary, focal point. You also want to have as much seating as possible face the TV. The easiest way to accomplish this is by putting the TV to the left or right of the primary focal point. This way your conversation area will incorporate the TV at the same time as facing the primary focal point. If the left or right of the primary focal point isn't possible, then place the TV on one of the walls perpendicular to the primary focal point.

BEFORE: *This family room emphasized the TV as the primary focal point. The room felt crowded and narrow.*

The Art of Redesign

AFTER: *By breaking my own rule about windows and putting the loveseat across the short side of the room, the primary focal point is now the bookcase with a beautiful piece of art over it. This is balanced by the second bookcase on the opposite wall. The TV is at an angle so it's not the first thing you see when you enter the room. The room is also more conversational, which will change the way the family uses the space.*

Sometimes the only place to put the TV is directly across from the primary focal point. In this case, there will be only one way to arrange your furniture — perpendicular to the primary focal point. That way people can look in one direction to see the primary focal point, and look the opposite way to see the TV.

BEFORE: *The homeowner had always wanted the fireplace to be the primary focal point in the room but in 15 years hadn't been able to figure out how to achieve that. The furniture blocked the entrance to the room, making it difficult to get to the table.*

AFTER: *Splitting up the white bookshelves allowed us to reorient the furniture toward the fireplace. Now it shines as the primary focal point in the room. Moving two of the bookshelves to the other side of the room helped balance the room.*

From a décor point of view, electronics are not attractive items. Whenever possible, hide your TV and other electronics in an armoire or other piece of furniture with doors. If you can't hide the TV, try to put it on a beautiful table or a small chest (or bureau if in a bedroom) rather than on the traditional particleboard TV stand. If your TV stand is attractive and works with the TV, then it can stay. Otherwise, try to find something that's at least attractive.

If your TV is in a three-piece entertainment center, it's going to be very difficult to balance the weight of that on the other side of the room. Try splitting the pieces so that you can distribute the weight around the room. If that's impossible, try using plants and/or art along with sofas and chairs, on the opposite side to help balance the room.

BEFORE: *Having three bookshelves together created a lot of heavy weight on one side of the room, which was difficult to balance on the other side of the room. The TV in the middle also meant that the furniture had to face the bookshelves instead of the fireplace.*

AFTER: *By splitting up the bookshelves we were able to move the television to the left of the fireplace. An easy guideline is to always place the TV as close to the left or right of the primary focal point as you can. That allows you to have a conversation area that addresses the primary focal point and the TV at the same time.*

There are some great stereo speakers that are so small they are almost invisible. Try to buy those. If you must have large stereo speakers, then center them or line them up with an architectural feature in the room. Never place anything on a speaker to make it 'look pretty.' This just draws attention to them. Angling them will also draw more attention to them, so place them straight on if possible.

CREATE A CONVERSATION GROUPING

Once you have placed those large pieces and the TV, then you will create a conversation grouping addressing (facing) the primary focal point.

Start with the largest sitting piece of furniture first — usually a sofa or loveseat. This piece of furniture will need to face the focal point in some way, shape or form.

Now the fun begins!

If the sofa/loveseat is going to face the primary focal point there are really only five spots it can go:

✹ Straight across from the focal point

✹ Perpendicular to the focal point to the left or right

✹ Angled to the left or right facing the focal point.

Obviously there are more than five — the angles can be anywhere: shallow, deep, or anything in between; but it simplifies the process to think of it as five options that you can try.

I like to try all five options and see what each one feels like. I'll try the sofa perpendicular on the left. If it feels like it could work, then I play with the other main seating pieces to see how I could arrange them if the sofa stayed there.

Then I'll try the sofa angled toward the fireplace from the left and play with the other pieces with the sofa in that spot.

I then move the sofa around the room trying the various options: straight across, angled from the right and perpendicular on the right.

By the time I've gone around the room doing this, usually one furniture arrangement jumps out as the best one.

One of the common mistakes I see is that if the room is unusually long, people tend to place the sofa along the longest wall. This just makes the room feel longer and narrower. Instead, place the sofa perpendicular to the longest wall or at a 45-degree angle to the longest wall. This will break up the long, 'hallway' feeling of the room and make it feel cozier and more balanced.

BEFORE: *This sofa was placed against the longest wall in the room. The result is a room that feels stiff and formal.*

AFTER: *Angling the sofa creates space for more seating in the room and a friendlier conversation area.*

Keep in mind the following guidelines when creating your conversation grouping:

✳ Whenever possible, do not place the sofa against a wall. A popular mistake people make is to place their furniture against the walls around the room. This causes two problems. First, you can't have a comfortable conversation in the room because you need to raise your voice to be heard. Second, the balance in the room is off because all the weight is around the perimeter of the room and there is no weight in the middle of the room. The goal is to have the weight of the furniture balanced throughout the room. Even if you can only bring the sofa out from the wall a foot or so, it will make the room feel more spacious and in better balance with the room.

Angling the sofa also creates the opportunity for pretty vignettes in the corners.

✳ Often a U-shaped conversation area works best. However, you can also make an L-shape. This will sometimes leave room to have a reading chair or a couple of chairs and a table in another area of the room, creating a separate seating area.

✳ Five or six people should be able to talk comfortably without bumping knees or having to raise their voices over too great a distance.

✳ Ideally everyone should be able to reach the coffee table.

✳ Furniture placed straight on to the focal point and 'squared up' tends to create rooms that give a more formal feel. The straightness tends to encourage people to imitate the symmetry in their body language and they will feel stiffer. Furniture angled towards the focal point, in contrast, will give a more pleasing informal feel to the room. So if you are trying to achieve a room with a more casual and comfortable feel, then try angling the furniture.

✷ Each large piece of furniture should be centered on or lined up with something around it, e.g. upholstered chairs might be lined up "foot-to-foot" with the sofa, or a bookcase might be centered on the space between the sofa and the outlying wall. Even if a sofa is centered on the fireplace, you can decide how close to put it by lining up the side of the sofa with the middle or the outside of a window or some other architectural feature of the room.

BEFORE: *The chairs were too far away from the sofa to have a comfortable conversation in this room.*

AFTER: *By bringing the chairs and sofas together facing the fireplace it's now possible to have an intimate conversation. The room feels more welcoming. Notice how the chair is centered on the fireplace. The sofas are lined up with the sides of the fireplace and the feet of the chair are lined up with the feet of the sofas.*

PLACING THE AREA RUG

Area rugs are a great way to bridge colors in a room. If you have two different colors, find an area rug with both colors in it. This will give a reason for the two different colors to be in the room.

An area rug also brings unity to the room and anchors the conversation area. Always try placing the conversation grouping without the area rug first, so you have all the available choices of furniture arrangements. If you're struggling with the furniture arrangement, take the furniture away and place the area rug; it will dictate furniture patterns and help you place the furniture. Always try the rug in different ways — horizontal to the primary focal point, vertical, and angled in two directions. You can get some wonderful surprises.

Rules to keep in mind are to relate the rug to the grouping and not float it alone in the center of the room. Also, make sure the rug is large enough for the space. There is a difference of opinion between decorators. Some say furniture should always be entirely on the rug or entirely off the rug — never half on and half off. Others say furniture should always have at least the front feet on the rug. So just play with your carpets and see what 'feels' better to you.

My experience is that most dining rooms have rugs that are too small. When placing a rug in a dining area, it should be at least six inches wider than the space a chair pulled back would take up. You need to be able to pull back your chair and still have all four legs of the chair on the rug. When in doubt always go up in size, not down.

I will often take the rug out of the dining room entirely if it's too small. I love the look of a wooden table on a hardwood floor, particularly if the wood colors contrast. Also, it's easier to keep clean.

PLACING THE REST OF THE FURNITURE

Once you have your conversation grouping you need to place the rest of the furniture and the large plants.

You will then need to place the other pieces of furniture such as cabinets and hutches.

When placing furniture in the room, think of creating triangles with the wooden pieces in the room. You can also think of this as creating Z's, or tacking (going left, right, left, right at an angle as they do in sailing or wind-surfing) when placing furniture in the room. Tacking or Z's is really just an extension of the triangle. You can also create a triangle of large plants. The objective is to have people (and their eyes) move throughout the room in an interesting manner. You don't want everything in a straight line.

On this side of the room there is a small triangle of wooden pieces with the demi-lune (half moon) table, the tea cart and the wooden chair.

On the other side of the room we have a triangle of wooden pieces comprised of the trunk, the table with the lamp, and the piano (barely visible on the right of the photo).

Put 'like with like'. Try to match colors of wood as much as possible. Many people don't realize that woods differ from each other in color. There are red woods, honey-gold woods, black ebony woods, chocolate-brown woods, and variations of these. You want to make sure that the wooden pieces in the room all work together and complement each other. If you have different colors of wooden pieces in the room, try to group them so they're not all seen at the same time. For example, you can have a corner with the honey-gold woods and then another corner with the darker woods.

Be sure there is enough wall space around each piece of furniture. Look at angling a piece in a corner if it's too tight on one wall. Try to leave a foot of space on either side of beautiful pieces of furniture or large plants you want to show off.

Never put one end of a piece of furniture in a corner. It will look cheap and unbalanced. Always center the piece on the wall or portion of wall on which it is positioned.

BEFORE: *Never shove furniture into a corner. It will make the room look small and the furniture will look cheap. In this case, the armoire was not only shoved into the corner, it went under a valance. When you have an architectural feature such as the valance in this room, the furniture must be either inside the valance or totally outside it.*

AFTER: *Moving the armoire to the center of the wall allowed the piece to shine. Also, we were then able to rearrange the furniture into a larger seating area, creating more space and better flow.*

Use large plants as if they were pieces of furniture. Use them to soften the sides of furniture, or to widen a piece of furniture on a wall, rather than putting them in a corner. They have much more impact that way. Rather than having plants all over the room, try grouping them for greater impact. If you group real plants and artificial plants together, they will all look real. When purchasing artificial plants, choose those with small leaves. They look more real than ones with large leaves.

The next step is to make sure that every person seated in the room has a table to place a cup of coffee, a drink, or a magazine. Some people will be able to reach the coffee table. Some will need an end table for this purpose. Sometimes it's more interesting if the end tables don't match, or if the coffee table is different from the end tables. They should still coordinate with each other, though.

Have a look at the coffee table in the room. Does the table now being used relate well to the sofa? If the sofa is very long, use a rectangular or elongated coffee table. Ideally it would be two-thirds the width of the sofa. Square tables are best placed in front of short sofas or loveseats.

If the current coffee table isn't working, try something else. There are numerous options for coffee tables:

✳ two low end tables put together

✳ an ottoman

✳ a bench

✳ an old steamer trunk or hope chest

✳ a higher round table used as a tea table (usually used with Victorian furniture)

✳ stacking tables placed side by side

✳ the coffee table being used in the family room

REMEMBER TO 'SHOP' IN YOUR HOME

Don't forget to shop in your home. If you don't have a sofa table, look for other things you can use. What about a small table with a plant beside it? Or a collection of plants? Perhaps you have a desk or a low piano that could act as a sofa table. Remember to 'think outside the box.'

BEFORE: *When you entered this room, the back of the sofa was uninviting.*

AFTER: *Adding the desk as a sofa table made a beautiful entrance into the room. It also added another function to the space.*

BALANCE THE ROOM

Pay attention to the balance in the room. For example, if you have a large fireplace at one end of the room, look at balancing it with a large piece such as an armoire on the opposite wall. Once the furniture is placed, stand in every corner of the room and check the balance of the room.

When you're looking at balance in a room, you want to look at the "visual weight" of items rather than the actual weight. For example, a bright red chair will carry a lot of visual weight in a room with all beige furniture. Patterns tend to carry more visual weight than solids. Elements which are visually forceful and attract our attention are things like unusual shapes, bright colors, dark values, and variegated textures. Smaller items that have these qualities can often balance larger items that do not.

BEFORE: *The bookcase was too heavy for the light furniture and windows on the other side of the room, making the room feel unbalanced.*

AFTER: *Taking the top off the cabinet and hanging light-colored art over it created the light, airy feeling that was required. The top was used as a bookcase in the bedroom.*

There are three types of balance:

SYMMETRICAL BALANCE

Symmetrical balance results from the arrangement of identical elements, corresponding in shape, size, and relative position, about a common line or axis. In a symmetrical arrangement, if you drew a line down the middle, both sides would be identical in weight. One side provides a "mirror" image of the other.

There are two types of symmetrical balance:

Bisymmetrical Balance (Formal)

Bisymmetrical balance is mirror-image balance. If you draw a line down the center of the arrangement, all the objects on one side are mirrored on the other side. They are completely identical. This is often seen in architecture.

Symmetrical Balance (Semi-Formal)

Symmetrical balance can be described as having equal "weight" on both sides of a centrally placed fulcrum. The weight is the same on both sides but the items are not identical.

ASYMMETRICAL BALANCE (CAN BE FORMAL OR INFORMAL)

Asymmetrical is more complex and difficult to envisage. It involves placement in a way that will allow objects of varying visual weight to balance one another around a fulcrum point. Although asymmetrical balance may appear more casual and less planned, it is usually harder to use because you must plan the layout very carefully to ensure that it is still balanced. An unbalanced arrangement creates a feeling of tension.

Asymmetry is recognized as the lack of correspondence in size, shape, color, or relative position among the elements of a composition. While a symmetrical composition requires the use of pairs of identical elements, an asymmetrical composition incorporates dissimilar elements.

For an asymmetrical arrangement to 'look' balanced the composition must take into account the visual weight of each of its elements. Elements which are visually forceful and attract our attention — unusual shapes, bright colors, dark values, and variegated textures — must be counterbalanced by less forceful elements which are larger. Or they must be placed farther away from the center of the composition. This means that if you draw a line down the middle, it would be different on either side, i.e. with different things on either side. You may even have different numbers of things on each side. However the whole thing would still have a symmetrically pleasing feel and look.

Asymmetrical balance is not as obvious as symmetry and is often more visually active and dynamic. It is capable of expressing movement and change and so tends to be more interesting to look at.

RADIAL BALANCE (CAN BE FORMAL OR INFORMAL)

The third type of balance is radial balance, where all elements radiate out from a center point in a circular fashion. It is very easy to maintain a focal point in radial balance, since all the elements lead your eye towards the center.

PAY ATTENTION TO THE 'LINES'

✳ Are all doors and windows clear? Tables or bureaus must go under a windowsill and not cross over it.

✳ If the furniture is crossing over wainscoting (panels in the wall) or bead-board, use a simple piece of furniture so there isn't a lot of 'busy-ness' for the eye to cope with. Never put a mirrored cabinet with shelves against wainscoting for this same reason. Also, when you put something in front of wainscoting you need to take the panels into account — put the furniture in the middle of the panels or line it up with one side of the panel or the other.

✳ Eliminate static lines when placing furniture and accessories. Create a variety of levels that keep the eye moving. You want the eye to gently flow from one piece to another.

✳ Avoid peaks and valleys as your eye travels around the room. You may need to soften tall pieces with a plant or a lamp or a piece of furniture that is mid-range from the top to the bottom of the tall piece. Balance low, medium, and tall items around the room and keep the movement between pieces gradual. For example, you wouldn't have a very small piece right next to a very tall piece. You would put something medium-sized in between them. When you're done, the eye should be able to gently undulate around the room between pieces.

FLOW

Look at the flow of the room. Are pathways functional and beautiful? Try to arrange the room so you can walk into it without being stopped by furniture or having to walk in front of people who are talking. Every room should invite you in, not stop you at the doorway.

Think about the kitchen or dining table. Are the table and chairs accessible from three or four sides? They probably are. What is true for your dining room or kitchen should also be true for your living room seating.

Take note of all the natural entries and the natural traffic patterns that the activities for the room will need. How do people use the room? If someone needs to leave for some reason, how do they get out? How do they get back to their seat? Can they do this easily without disturbing other people in the room? Make it as easy as possible for people to move in the room.

There should be traffic lanes into the room, around the room, leading to other rooms, and leading up to windows. A good rule of thumb is to allow two to three feet of width in passageways. If someone is moving between two items with sharp corners at hip height, you will want the passage to be wider. If the items are soft, or are below knee height, then the passage can be narrower. Also pay attention to the height where someone with broad shoulders could bump into something.

WATCH FOR INVISIBLE WALLS

Watch for invisible walls that are formed by the room's architecture, such as in an L-shaped living room/dining room. You want to make sure that furniture is all on one side of the invisible wall or the other, not crossing it. If there's a railing or a half-wall in the room, there is an invisible line that extends from the railing or half-wall, creating an invisible wall that has to be worked with.

You can deliberately create invisible walls using a long sofa, a tall backless bookcase or étagère, or two or three large plants or trees.

BEFORE: *These homeowners loved to cook and their friends loved to watch. But the furniture was lined up in a row facing the kitchen — not very inviting or conversational.*

AFTER: *Turning the sofa divided the space into two distinct rooms. Now they have a great conversation area near the kitchen as well as the living room. Guests can speak with each other as well as the chefs in the kitchen. Don't be afraid to use all the floor-space. Furniture doesn't need walls to hold it up.*

LARGE LIVING ROOMS

If you have a large living room, consider making more than one conversation area. Or have a conversation area and a separate space for reading. You could also have a separate space with a small table and two chairs.

BEFORE: *This living room was very large so the homeowner tried to stretch the furniture, ignoring the primary focal point (the fireplace) in the process. When she had guests over, she was always bringing in chairs from the dining room.*

AFTER: *We brought in her loveseat which had been 'stored' in the guestroom. Then we arranged the furniture in a nice conversation area using the fireplace as a primary focal point. There was still room to create a separate space for reading in her favorite spot — a corner with a view of the pool.*

DINING ROOMS

A dining room needs a primary focal point too. Usually it's art over a hutch or a buffet. Even just a large piece of punchy art can be the primary focal point in the room. Experiment with making the dining room table larger. Often it actually makes the dining room look bigger rather than smaller.

Play with different places for the table. Try horizontal, vertical, and angled to the left or to the right. Even though you may not think it will look good initially, you can get some interesting surprises if you try things.

BEFORE: *The many plants and the outdated carpet made the room feel old and tired. Also, the wall that the cabinet was on ended just above the cabinet, so the china cabinet was too high for that particular wall. We moved the cabinet to the other side of the room where the wall was higher, going all the way to the ceiling.*

AFTER: *We created a focal point in the room with a buffet and art. Notice how the two pictures on the left extend the width of the focal point. Removing the outdated rug and some of the plants gave the room an updated look.*

Also pay attention to windows in the dining room, just as you did in the living room. It's nice if you can walk up to them.

Look at the scale of the furniture in the room. Balance is important in every room in the home.

If you decide to make a great-room or living room into a dining room, don't go part way. Let the table take center stage just as it would in a traditional dining room.

Look at the placement of the china cabinet in the room. Many dining rooms have an alcove designed for the china cabinet. However, often the china cabinet just fits and there is no 'space' around it to show it off. If there isn't a foot of space around your china cabinet when it's in the alcove, consider taking it out and putting it on another wall in the room where it can shine.

BEFORE: *The hutch in this room was blocking the window. In addition, the table placement made the room feel small.*

AFTER: *Moving the hutch to the other wall opened up the window, creating light and space. Turning the table and the area rug also opened up the room. Plus now we could hang a beautiful piece of art over the hutch, creating a lovely focal point in the room.*

BEFORE: *The computer desk was too small to balance the huge china cabinet on the other side of the room. It was also out of scale with the dining table. Functionally, it wasn't working well either.*

AFTER: *The height and weight of the bookcase worked so much better in the space. The books and ornaments brought warmth and life to the room as well. The computer desk was moved into the living room/family room. Now the person working at it could be with the rest of the family, which they all loved.*

Or look at the possibility of putting the china cabinet in another room. China cabinets can work well in a living room, family room, or large foyer if there is not enough room for them in the dining room. Display items in the china cabinet that work with the room. Art objects or books might be more appropriate.

If you take the china cabinet out of the alcove put a hutch, buffet table, or other pretty table there instead. Add a gorgeous piece of art over it and you'll be amazed at how beautiful your dining room will look.

BEFORE: *This open concept dining room led to a living room with sleek, modern lines. The china cabinet was out of place with the clean lines of the other furniture.*

AFTER: *Removing the top of the china cabinet gave the room the same sleek look of the living room. It also allowed us to highlight the artwork of the homeowner's daughter.*

What if you have an old traditional dining room set that you're tired of, but you can't afford a new one? Consider taking the top off the china cabinet. Use only the bottom of it as a hutch, and hang a gorgeous piece of art over it. This is the quickest way I know to update a dining room. And it also provides you with serving space.

What to do with the top? Maybe it can stand alone as a low bookcase or curio cabinet in the family room or the bedroom. Perhaps you can hang it on a wall for storage in the basement or garage. Play and let your creativity work for you.

BEFORE: *The sitting room had a single loveseat straight across from a chest. The room felt sparse and cold.*

AFTER: *We used the top of the china cabinet as a bookcase and angled the furniture. The room felt warm and cozy. Two people could now comfortably watch television or read a book. More importantly, you can now have a conversation in this room.*

BEDROOMS

The primary focal point in the bedroom is the bed. A great position for the bed is the wall across from the entrance to the room. You can also place the bed facing the door from the diagonal. In other words, place it on one of the two far walls to the left or right of the entrance. These positions give the person in bed visual command of the room and entrance when they are awake. You don't want to be sleeping with your back to the door, as there's a subliminal discomfort in knowing that someone could come in at night behind you.

Try to put a seating area in the bedroom. Even if you never sit there, it adds a feeling of comfort and relaxation to the room.

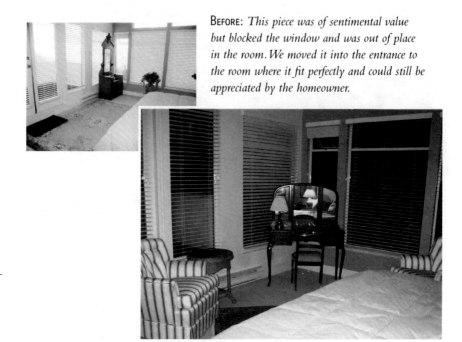

BEFORE: *This piece was of sentimental value but blocked the window and was out of place in the room. We moved it into the entrance to the room where it fit perfectly and could still be appreciated by the homeowner.*

AFTER: *Moving the dressing table now allows the homeowner to look out at the view as she gets ready for work. The seating area has given the homeowners a spot to read or have a conversation. It also makes the room feel cozy.*

The master bedroom, above all other rooms, must be your sanctuary. If you're going to get rid of clutter anywhere, this is the room. You should be able to walk into your bedroom and have the weight of the world fall off your shoulders. This is your refuge, your haven, the one spot where you can totally relax.

BEFORE: *The dressing table felt small and insignificant against this wall and the room felt out of balance.*

AFTER: *Adding a piece of furniture with more weight fixed the balance issues in the room and highlighted this beautiful piece of furniture.*

BEFORE: *This bedroom had too many small pieces. Also, the open shelving makes the room feel cluttered.*

AFTER: *Removing the clutter and putting solid pieces together gives the room a feeling of peace and tranquility. Now the beautiful view out the window is highlighted, rather than the clutter in the room.*

OFFICES

As in bedrooms, you want the person sitting at the desk to have visual command of the room and the door. The best position is to be facing the door when you're seated at the desk. The next best alternative is to have the door on your left or right. If you are working or studying with your back to the door, you will not be as relaxed or as focused as when you can see who is entering at all times. If the desk must be there, hang a mirror to reflect the doorway so you can see if someone is entering the room.

BEFORE: *The desk in this office was small and uninviting. This homeowner worked from home and had to look at a wall and have her back to the room for a lot of hours.*

AFTER: *Imagine how it felt to have her desk face the room. She can also now look outside to the garden through the patio doors (to the left bottom corner of the photo). The white cabinet behind the desk was at the other end of the room with nothing in it. They were planning to get rid of it because they didn't know what to use it for. Look at the function she has in her home office now.*

Don't worry about cords showing. You can group them together with Velcro strips to make them tidy and perhaps put a plant in front of the desk to hide them. It's more important for the person sitting at the desk to be comfortable than to worry about wires showing.

BASEMENTS

Basements tend to be ignored when it comes to creating a cozy inviting space. This is often where members of the family spend a great deal of time so it's important to make it feel good. It doesn't take much. Even inexpensive furniture can look great if it's placed properly.

BEFORE: *The homeowner had done a renovation and the basement family room got the leftover furniture.*

AFTER: *But what a difference you can make with just a little thought. Now it's possible to watch television and have a conversation in this great-looking room. And yes, they already had this entertainment unit but weren't using it for the TV.*

THE FOYER

The foyer or entrance into your home is your first impression spot. The foyer should be friendly, inviting and functional. Try to keep clutter out of the entrance. You don't want to be faced with chaos when you get home from work. You should be able to walk in and feel like you've come home to your haven.

BEFORE: *This foyer had too much "stuff." Even the art was 'off.' You don't want to come home feeling like there's work to be done.*

AFTER: *Ah, calm. This is a nice place to come home to.*

BEFORE: *This foyer was a bit cold and sparse.*

AFTER: *Now it's warm and inviting, with a space to sit and take off your shoes. This is a very eclectic combination of art and furniture. However, the colors in the art were bright gold and blue, which mimicked the colors in the chair seat and the pottery on the chest. When you have furnishings of different styles and periods, they must have a commonality that joins them together. In this case it was color.*

LET THERE BE LIGHT

After finishing the furniture placement, the next step is to place the lighting in the room.

The lighting in the room should happen at three levels:

AMBIENT LIGHTING

For uniform light throughout the room, create a triangle with the placement of your lamps. If you have only two lights, a diagonal is better than a straight line as it will cover more of the room.

TASK LIGHTING

Consider task lighting to ensure there is the right kind of light for the activities in the room. If you have a reading chair, make sure there's a lamp beside it. If you have a desk, you need a lamp on it. If you are sewing or doing crafts you will need appropriate lighting. Good task lighting should be behind the reader's shoulder and the shade should be slightly below the reader's nose. Do not place a reading lamp square in the center of an end table near a sofa or chair. Bring it toward the upholstery and closer to the reader.

ACCENT LIGHTING

Look at using lighting to highlight special items. Put a light shining up through plants or trees to illuminate the foliage. Use lights to highlight special pieces of art or statues.

Following are a few general guidelines to use when incorporating lighting into your room.

* If your lamp is not tall enough, elevate it on hardback books with the dust jackets removed.

* If you have two matching lamps, elevate one of them by placing a couple of books under it, for added interest. The elevated lamp should generally be at the left of the sofa. We "read" a room like we read a book — left to right.

✳ Chandeliers are often too high in a dining room. The guideline is about 36 inches above the table. Obviously if the chandelier is very large it will need to be higher than that.

STEP BACK AND OBSERVE

That's the furniture! Look around the room. It should feel balanced, harmonious, and cozy. There should be a lovely conversation area that you want to sit in. Take a look from each corner of the room. How does it feel? Check the flow. Can people easily enter and exit the room in order to use it the way it's meant to be used? What about functionality? Does everyone have a place to put down a drink or a magazine? Is the favorite TV-watching chair facing the TV? Is there a lamp by the reading chair?

At this point the room should already feel great. If it doesn't, then you need to look at your placement of furniture again.

Is there too much furniture on one side of the room, and not much on the other? Do you have an even distribution of the wooden pieces throughout the room? What about the plants? Think of putting three wooden pieces in a triangle in the room. Or maybe you need a triangle of plants. Maybe your conversation area is just a bit off and you need to adjust your angles or line up the chairs with the sofa better. Keep playing until you love the furniture arrangement and it 'feels' good. Placing the furniture properly is the most important thing you can do to make a room balanced, harmonious, and functional. Once the furniture is properly placed, the rest of your design will follow. I see so many people who buy new art and accessories trying to make their rooms work. It can't happen if the furniture isn't right first.

However, now that we've placed the furniture, and the room feels great, we can move on to art!

The Art of Redesign

STEP
4 | Walls

Choosing where to hang the art in a room is often such a daunting task that people avoid it for months. So let's find a way to make it fun.

When I'm teaching, we try everything, even when we believe it won't work. When I hold up a picture in a certain spot and it's right, everyone in the class knows instantly. I can feel the energy in the room change. They say "Yes!" "I love it!" "That's great there!" That's when I know it's the right place for that picture. You will know it too. You just need to trust yourself.

You will always know when something is right. You just need to play with putting things in different places until you feel what I call the "Yes!" factor. Assume you put something in a spot and you step back to look at it. 'It's okay ... it's all right ... it's not that bad,' you think. If that's what you're thinking, then it's not good enough. When you step back to look at it, your first reaction should be "Yes!" That's when you know it's right.

You also need to follow the steps and trust the system. Believe me. It works. I never know what a home will look like when I start. I just follow the system and magic happens. That's what makes redesign so exciting.

I first met Joe when he called me to redesign his condo after he had separated from his wife. He was now living by himself and wanted his place to look and feel like a home. It was one of the more difficult redesigns we'd done because he didn't have a lot to work with. For example, we had hung a picture over the mantel that was actually a bit smaller than the size and scale we would have preferred. However, it was the only one we had. So we needed accessories on the mantel to 'beef it up.' I searched everywhere for something that would be appropriate in the few accessories he had. Finally, I climbed up on his kitchen counter and found a small pink vase in the top right-hand corner of the farthest cupboard. Now I needed something to put in it to give me height. Since he lived in a condominium complex, the grounds were all perfectly pruned and I knew I couldn't cut any greenery from there. So I crossed the street and cut a few stray twigs with unopened cherry blossoms from the tree there. The pinkish-red of the twigs complemented the little vase perfectly. Finally, I had a mantel that was acceptable.

Joe was thrilled with his redesign and, frankly, we were too.

Over the next few years, Joe's mother passed away and he and his father, Ralph, sold their respective homes and bought a beautiful condo near a golf course. They called me to redesign it. I had thought that Joe was one of the nicest men I'd ever met, but Ralph went beyond that. I have never met a kinder, more interesting man in my life. We loved him from the moment we met him. Ralph had been an aeronautical engineer in his younger days but had always painted as a hobby. He had dozens of stunning paintings, predominantly of boats and planes.

Sadly, just prior to the big move, Ralph was diagnosed with terminal cancer. He and Joe requested that we hang as much of Ralph's art as we possibly could so he could appreciate it.

Normally the client is away when we do a redesign but with Ralph's condition he needed to be home where he was comfortable. Wanting to surprise him, we had him wait in the den until we had hung the art. Joe was familiar with the process and I knew his presence would be helpful so he got to stay as well.

We decided to create a gallery of Ralph's paintings of boats in the living room where he could easily see them. We artfully arranged the paintings in collections that worked with the furniture. From his chair he could see the fireplace with a gorgeous painting over the mantel, as well as the entertainment center for the TV. We hung his art across the top of the entertainment center and down both sides, which was quite dramatic. When he looked left or right, he could see even more of his art strategically hung.

From his chair he could also see a large wall of the dining room. We did a collection of six of his large paintings of planes on that wall.

When Ralph walked into the living room, this wonderful ninety-year-old man actually started to giggle with glee. We had him sit in his chair and he couldn't stop smiling and thanking us.

We carried on with the rest of the home and the accessorizing. I unpacked a box and there, gently wrapped in newspaper, were the twigs I had cut for Joe's mantel. "Joe, what is this?" He came into the room, looked at the twigs, and replied, "Those are for my mantel." I was so touched that I had to gulp back a sob. I found the little pink vase, put the twigs in it, and placed it on the mantel where, once again, it was the perfect touch.

We finished the redesign, which Joe and Ralph absolutely loved. There were many hugs and expressions of gratitude. I can't explain how rewarding it felt to give these two wonderful men such a gift. The moment that I will never forget, though, was when Ralph walked me to the front door. He held my hand, looked into my eyes, and softly said, "You've given us a home."

———————

HANGING ART

So you've placed the furniture, large plants, tables, area rugs, and the lighting. Now it's time to incorporate wall art. While the furniture placement is critical and sets the foundation for the whole home, the artwork brings personality and 'soul' to the room.

Bring all of the artwork back into the room from your holding or staging area. For the purposes of redesign, art is anything that can be placed on a wall. This means that in addition to pictures, it includes things like plates, hats, baskets, wall reliefs, shelves, sconces, and quilts.

This grouping was done by theme and color. The table top has the same colors as the wooden carving above it. This makes the contemporary piece work. Also, the frames and matting of the art are contemporary.

Note: when you're moving your art around, pick it up by the wire, especially oils and fine art. This ensures you don't get oil from your fingers on the art. It also ensures that the wire is strong enough to hold the picture. (It's better to find out before you hang it.)

Lean the wall art against furniture around the room so you can view all of it.

Now look at the art in terms of grouping it. Which pictures would form a nice collection? Which could be a set? Put like with like and sort the pictures that way. You can make a collection of art that all has the same colors, or the same theme (for example, landscapes), or similar shapes (for abstract art).

We had placed this sewing machine in the foyer and then a chair beside it for function. So what art to hang? We found a number of black and white pieces that pick up the black in the sewing machine. They work well as a collection, even though the themes and styles are very different.

Following are some tips for grouping art:

✳ Group art with matching frames or coordinated frames as much as possible. Just as in furniture, there are wooden frames with honey-gold coloring, frames with dark wood, and frames with red wood. Try to separate these so you don't have multiple colors of wooden frames in your collection. Look at putting gold with gold and silver/pewter with silver/pewter.

✳ Group art that uses the same medium. Put oil paintings with oil paintings and watercolors with watercolors. Do not mix photographs, oil paintings, and watercolors in the same collection. The exception to this is if they all have the same theme. For example, you can mix mediums if all the pictures are landscapes or horses.

✳ Pairs are great. Not only do they complement each other but they also add balance and rhythm to a room. They should be matted and framed identically and hung at the same level with their bottoms flush or one directly on top of the other. Don't stagger them. Pictures should never be staggered unless you have a reason to stagger them, such as hanging art going up a staircase or over a triangular piece of furniture, or to offset accessories or lamps.

Now that we have our art sorted into pairs and collections, we need to look around the room and find places that seem bare and require art.

Begin with the focal wall in the room to make the most impact with what you have. Then choose the second most important spot, and so on.

In the art of redesign, this may mean you have empty spaces after you have used all the art. That's okay. Don't try to "stretch" the art to fill the room. Focus on each area and make it the best it can be. If there are empty areas when done, then you may have an excuse to do a little shopping to finish the space. On the other hand, it's sometimes nice to have some empty walls in a room so the eye can rest. It's a beautiful counterpoint to the walls that do have art. Just make sure the empty wall isn't the largest wall in the room. The room still needs to feel balanced.

When you have a primary focal point in the room (like a fireplace), you want to reinforce it. This is the most important spot in the room so you want to start here while you still have all the art to choose from. Find a piece or collection that works with the tiles or bricks in the fireplace. The colors should complement each other, with the art making the fireplace look good and the fireplace returning the favor to the art.

BEFORE: *The art and accessories were taking away from the architecturally beautiful windows and built-in cabinets.*

AFTER: *When you have beautiful architectural features, you don't want to compete with them. Instead, keep it simple. The roundness of the pottery plate and the vase are a nice counterpoint to all the square lines and pick up the curves in the windows and the top of the leaded glass bookshelves.*

Usually a fireplace needs something hung over it, even if there is no mantel. Exceptions are elaborate brick or stone fireplaces or fireplaces with a rounded or unusually shaped flue. The roundness, the architectural shape, or the texture is the decoration. Never try to hang a picture on a curved surface. It will make both the curved surface and the picture look odd.

Sometimes a picture looks best propped against the wall over the mantel rather than hung. Or you can hang one picture on the wall and prop a smaller, related picture nearby. Always try propped and hung options to see which works best. There is no 'right or wrong.' There's only 'what I like' and 'what I don't like.'

Now you get to play again. Try art that you think won't work to see if you're right or not. Layer art. Layer pictures on top of mirrors. Use objects as art. Have fun. Your eye will tell you when something is working or not working, and if your eye doesn't tell you, your friend will.

This homeowner didn't have a large piece of art that worked with her fireplace. We solved the problem by layering a number of smaller pieces and incorporating accessories.

While I know it's popular to put a large mirror over the mantel, I'm not a big fan of that option. When you think about it, a mirror is just a frame around a blank hole if it doesn't reflect anything. Usually in a living room or family room that 'hole' just reflects the white ceiling — not that attractive and does nothing for the balance of the room. Art has much more impact and visual appeal than a mirror reflecting the ceiling.

Having said that, a beautiful mirror with a large bouquet of flowers or greenery in front of it is fabulous. Then it becomes art and you get double flowers or greenery. Another nice option is if you tilt the mirror forward from the top so that it reflects gorgeous artwork or a beautiful piece of furniture on the other side of the room. You can do this with a piece of cork or a few felt pads stuck together.

So only put a mirror over the mantel if the fireplace is directly across from something that needs to be reflected, like a pretty view or a beautiful piece of furniture. Even then, often a mirror does not give the color or warmth that some rooms need.

BEFORE: *The large mirror over the fireplace was out of scale and the frame had no commonality with the fireplace or anything else in the room.*

AFTER: *We found a mirror that worked with the colors in the fireplace, however it was too small. So we layered a piece of art with similar colors and added accessories. Now the colors work with the fireplace and the rest of the room.*

Think of hanging art to work in conjunction with the furniture and ornaments around it. Art should be hung to show the pieces off to their best advantage while keeping them in harmony with the rest of the room. You want to use the art to enhance the furniture it's around rather than just hanging it to fill space on the wall.

BEFORE: *In the dining room, the picture was too small for the space and didn't have any commonality with the dark side table.*

AFTER: *This was the perfect spot for the mirror from the living room. The scale and frame worked perfectly with the side table, the dining table, and the kitchen counter. The mirror also reflected some beautiful art pieces on the opposite wall*

In one home the client had a huge wall in the dining room that needed two or three large pieces of art in order to work with the scale of the wall. However, the client didn't own any art of the right size and shape. Rather than hanging art in the middle of the wall where it would look too small, we hung a vertical piece of art beside a huge palm tree on one side of the wall, and then made a collection of furniture, accessories, and art on the other side of the wall. We had a small chest that was quite narrow. To visually increase the width, we found a brass wine bucket on a stand that worked with the brass in the chest. We staggered two pieces of art with gold and silver in them over the width of the chest and wine cooler combined. Then we put accessories on the chest that worked with the artwork and wine bucket. The effect was fabulous. There was a blank space in the middle of the wall, but when you looked left you saw a beautiful vignette and when you looked right you saw another beautiful vignette. The wall was still balanced and so was the room.

Think of using art, furniture, and accessories together to fill space.

If at all possible, try never to hang one piece of art floating on a wall by itself. You get more impact if you hang a pair, or hang a collection of art. If you hang just one piece, hang it over a table or other piece of furniture. Even putting a shelf under a piece of art has more impact than having art just floating on a wall. Obviously the exception would be a large canvas with rich or bright colors. In that case, the visual weight is strong enough by itself.

BEFORE: *These pictures were hung too high. Your eye is drawn to the space between the furniture and the art, rather than to the art. Also, the pictures weren't grouped to work with each other or to work with the furniture.*

AFTER: *The homeowner had wonderful art scattered throughout the home. We grouped all the art with the same theme and hung it in a collection over the sofas. Notice how your eye is now drawn to the beautiful art and how it enhances the look of the furniture.*

BEFORE: *Try to avoid having a picture floating on a wall by itself. It has much more impact if it's hung in a pair, a grouping, or over a piece of furniture.*

AFTER: *Notice how the two pictures over the buffet have much more impact than the single small picture. Also, the delicate leaves in the vase work with the delicate artwork. The picture hanging by itself on the other wall had strong primary colors, so was strong enough to hang by itself and balance the weight on the other side of the room.*

CREATING A GROUPING

When creating a grouping in an area, lay it out on the floor beneath the space to get a feel for the composition you are trying to achieve. For grouping art I recommend laying out your display on a non-patterned surface like a neutral carpet or a sheet on the bed before you start putting nails in the wall. Or you can cut out pieces of paper the same size as the picture and tape them on the wall.

Pay close attention to the components of the grouping. They should relate either by subject or color. Observe placement of dark and light frames as well as matting colors. You are trying to achieve a sense of balance by mixing the colors throughout the grouping.

Groupings or single pictures should occupy about two-thirds of the space of the piece of furniture they are hanging over to achieve the proper proportion.

When hanging a grouping:

✳ The pieces in the group should be hung closely enough together so that when you stand back and look at the group you can see the outer geometric shape that they form.

✳ Keep pictures within the grouping fairly close together with no large, obvious gaps. Otherwise, the grouping starts to look disjointed. If you find you have a large gap, consider putting in a small picture or some kind of ornament that can be hung with fishline.

✳ A good rule of thumb is to space wall art about a palm's width (2-3 inches) apart. This visually relates the items. If the pictures are small or visually very light, then decrease the space between pictures. If they are large or visually heavy, then you may want to increase the space between pictures. Often you can use the width of the matting as a guideline as well.

✳ An odd number is usually best for a grouping.

✳ Look at your grouping on the floor first. Make sure strong colors are evenly distributed.

✳ Pictures with people in them should have the person looking into the grouping, not away from the grouping. In fact, this applies to anything with 'eyes.' The eyes need to be looking into the grouping so that it remains cohesive.

BEFORE: *The single picture over this sofa was hung too high and both the scale of the picture and the size were out of proportion to the sofa. Ideally you want the art to be 2/3 the width of the piece over which you're hanging it and never wider than the piece. The statue and candles on the mantle didn't work with the fireplace, making the items look wrong and the fireplace look bad.*

AFTER: *We found a collection of art that had the same color tones as the sofa. Note how a collection has much more impact than the single picture. The art over the mantle had the same color tones as the brick in the fireplace. Now everything works together.*

WHAT HEIGHT TO HANG IT?

The biggest and most frequent question I'm asked is how high to hang the art or the collection of art. Everyone has heard the phrase "hang the art at eye level." I'd like to know who came up with that one. Whose eye level are we using ... the six-foot husband's or the five-foot wife's?

The reality is that art is viewed from a seated position, except in a hallway or foyer. So consider the function of the room. Generally art will be hung a lot lower in rooms such as the dining room or living room where people are sitting so they can appreciate it while seated. Place art higher in hallways and places where people are standing.

As previously mentioned, hang art to work with the furniture. When placing artwork over a piece of furniture such as a sofa or a table, hang it no higher than six to eight inches over the furniture. Sometimes even four or five inches works better. If the picture or collection of art is too high, the eye is drawn to the gap between the art and the furniture. If it's too low, the eye is drawn to the ceiling. You want the art to relate to the furniture. If you are hanging art over a table where you intend to place accessories, you may hang the art higher or lower depending on which accessories you will be placing on the table.

BEFORE: *None of these items had any commonality. The contemporary mirrors didn't work with the art above them or the chest and accessory below.*

AFTER: *The golden tones in the chest were picked up in the art and the accessories. The pictures were hung lower, to work with the chest. The walls beside this vignette were left blank, so as not to compete with it.*

All art has a focal point, usually in the top third or bottom third of the picture. If the focal point is in the top third, the eye will travel up easier than if the focal point is low in the picture. This means that you can hang the art a little lower. When the focal point is in the lower third of the picture you can hang the art a little higher.

Watch the visual weight of the art. If the art (or the mat and frame) is dark or visually heavy, leave more space between the art and the sofa.

For art on walls viewed from a standing position, hang it so that the middle of the picture is 55 to 58 inches from the floor. You may want to take into account the heights of the people who live there as well. If everyone in the family is tall, you may hang the art at the higher end of the range. Just remember that you want the main part of the image — particularly the focal point of the art — to be easily viewed by most people.

Here's a tip: when in doubt, hang art lower rather than higher. Then, if you have to move it up, the art will hide the hole.

If you're hanging a pair of pictures vertically, it's generally better to put the visually heavier piece on the bottom. But don't be afraid to break some rules. Sometimes doing the opposite will give the pair a more interesting look.

Look at tucking artwork into unusual places such as between the lamp table and lampshade, or low along a pony wall (half-wall). This will create a nice surprise for the eyes.

Use art to expand a piece of furniture. If you have a vertically narrow piece of furniture that's too small for a wall, adding artwork on the side of it can expand the size and soften the strong vertical line. By adding a plant or tree to the other side (or more art) you have now created a wide 'piece of furniture' that properly fills the space.

The china cabinet was too small for the alcove in this dining room. The homeowner had placed a chair beside it but it still looked wrong. Also, the carving over the alcove made the furniture taller and more narrow.

AFTER: *By placing art and accessories beside the cabinet to widen it, the size works. Also, note that a mirror was hung to the right. A piece of art there would have competed with the art in the dining room. Unbeknownst to us, the homeowner had been looking for a new china cabinet the whole time we were redesigning her home. When she saw her 'new' dining room, she said, "I don't need a new china cabinet anymore. You just saved me $5,000!"*

Think of giving art breathing space. As I mentioned, leaving one wall in every room free of art to give the eye a resting place is often preferable to surrounding people with art. Ensure your art has enough "white space" around it to show it off. Avoid hanging two pieces of art on adjacent walls at a corner. They will only compete with each other and you won't be able to appreciate either. The exception would be if you are creating a corner vignette with two chairs and a table. In that case, a pair works well.

If you have two small walls on either side of your fireplace, the art on either side must work with the art over the fireplace as a collection. This visually expands the focal point and is very powerful. If you don't have art that works with the art over the mantel, you need to enhance those spaces with something else that won't compete with it. Consider putting a large plant on one side or a smaller plant with a mirror. Other things that work well are wall reliefs, sconces, or items that have the same theme as the art and work with it. An example of this would be African artifacts hung on the wall beside an African painting. Fish-line works great for hanging artifacts. I've strung fish-line through the nostrils or eyeballs of masks, or tied it around the neck. (Kind of gory if you have a good imagination but it works.)

BEFORE: *The art on either side of the fireplace was competing with the art over the mantle, causing the room to feel disjointed.*

AFTER: *Using plants on one side and a chest with accessories on the other enhanced the piece of art over the fireplace instead of competing with it. The rich dark colors in this new piece of art worked better with the weight of the furniture in this room as well. Note that two end tables put together can make a gorgeous coffee table. Now everyone has a place to put down their glass or cup.*

AFTER *(Dining Room): The art previously over the fireplace was stunning in the dining room over a table with similar pewter tones.*

To eliminate glare, place a small piece of cork between the upper center of the frame and the wall. This will tilt the picture slightly.

Always use two hooks for medium to large art. This will ensure that the piece hangs correctly. The hooks never need to be more than one foot apart.

If you have a heavy piece to hang on drywall you will need to use a plug or screw anchor. There are two ways to use screw anchors or plugs in drywall:

1. Take out your drill. Drill a hole a bit smaller than the width of your plug; punch in the plug with your hammer; screw in the screw.

2. Use an awl or other pointed object to make the hole. An awl is a great tool. It's also useful for starting holes when you're re-wiring a picture. An awl has a small round handle attached to a piece of pointed metal. To make a hole, place the awl in the wall and hit it with a hammer. Turn the awl around a few times to enlarge the hole. Pound in the anchor and then screw in the screw.

Hanging art going up a staircase is one of the few instances where art will be at different heights (staggered). The angle of the grouping should be the same as the angle of the stairs. A rule of thumb is to place the bottom of the image approximately 55 inches above the step where it will hang.

If there are lots of windows and no wall space, look at propping art on tables with stands or putting art on easels.

SUNSHINE AND HUMIDITY

Canvas, no glass; Paper, always glass. That is probably the easiest way to think about how art is mounted. When an artist paints on canvas they generally treat it such that it can be hung anywhere. They don't often use watercolors on canvas, mostly acrylics or oils, so I don't think it will be something that you will come up against.

Oil paintings should be fine no matter where you hang them, as they won't fade in sun and humidity isn't an issue. However, watercolors or pastels will need to be hung out of direct sunlight to avoid fading. They are also subject to humidity so avoid hanging them in bathrooms, kitchens, or over a fish tank where humidity is high. Usually a powder room is safe as the humidity isn't as high as it would be with a bath or shower in the room.

Limited editions or oils on paper should be 'museum-' or 'conservation'-framed. This means that nothing with acid touches the art and the glass has UVA protection.

Think about rotating art in summer and winter if sunshine is a concern. Or just hang sun-sensitive art on darker walls.

WALL ART IS MORE THAN PICTURES

MIRRORS

When you are considering hanging a mirror, think about why you would hang it in a certain spot. There are four reasons to hang a mirror:

1. To reflect something attractive.
2. To be useful, like near the front door, over a dresser in a bedroom or, if it is a long vertical, in a hallway where you can check your clothing.

3.   To add light to a dark spot in the room.

4.   To increase the size of the room.

Be careful about hanging mirrors just to make the room look bigger. A cozy, intimate room is preferable to a cold room with a wall full of mirror reflecting a white wall.

You only want to expand the size of the room if you are reflecting something beautiful. I love doubling the greenery from the window, or a piece of beautiful art, or a gorgeous Oriental armoire, but twice as much white wall is not a good thing.

Think about what the mirror will reflect at night as well as during the day. It's great to reflect a beautiful view, but when the curtains are closed, do you want two sets of curtains in the room? Would beautiful art be better?

If the entire wall over a mantel is mirrored, consider having it removed. It will mostly reflect the ceiling and creates a huge blank space over the mantel.

If you can't remove it, then choose some dramatically beautiful accessories to place in front of the mirror. Greenery from the garden can fill empty space and make the humblest vase look elegant. Another option is to hang a picture from the ceiling or prop one or two pictures on the mantel to minimize the amount of mirror.

You can buy sticky, rubbery 'tack' to stick the top of the picture to the mirror and the bottom to the mantel to prevent the art from slipping. You can also buy round rubber 'bumpers' that you can put on the mantel to stop the picture from sliding forward.

Look for very large sculptural pieces to put on the mantel, or even hang from the ceiling. Get creative. The objective is to have something interesting over the mantel for you to look at instead of a wall of mirror.

If you have many mirrors and not much art, find something pretty to place in front of the hung mirrors so that the reflected vignettes appear to be art. A gorgeous vase of flowers or greenery, or a beautiful sculpture in front of a mirror is fabulous.

PLATES

Hang plates as you would pictures, making sure they relate to the theme of the room. They are most attractive hung alongside a china cabinet and are usually appropriate for a dining room or kitchen.

QUILTS OR FABRIC

A beautiful quilt, tapestry, rug, or piece of fabric can bring color and interest to a room. How to hang?

* use small nails right through the fabric

* staple a piece of Velcro across the wall, sew the matching strip of Velcro to the quilt, and hang.

* make a sleeve for the quilt or fabric and purchase a dowel to go through the sleeve for hanging.

* attach tacking for carpets to a piece of wood with little nails. Hang the quilt on the tacking. This works well for hanging rugs and tapestries as well.

ORIENTAL SCREENS

If you are hanging an Oriental screen for the first time, and there is no hardware for the screen, put heavy-duty mirror hangers on the back. You can also use L-shaped brackets. Consider splitting the screen and hanging one, two, or three panels as art instead.

MASKS

Masks and other unusual art pieces can usually be hung using fishline. Be sure to make a square knot (reef knot) so the art will be secure. As I learned in Girl Guides when I was a child, to tie this knot, simply hold one piece of fishline in each hand. Put right over left, tuck under and pull, then left over right, tuck under and pull. I usually put two or three knots in it to be safe.

I have to tell you another quick story. When I did the consultation for one client's home, he had pointed out a stack of pictures they had purchased when they were in Thailand. "It would be nice if these could be hung somewhere," he said.

It turned out that the colors in these eight pictures worked beautifully with his rust-colored loveseat in the den. I carefully laid the pictures out on the floor and arranged them according to color, putting the vertical pieces on the inside and the horizontal pieces on the outside. Then I made sure the balance felt right. We hung all eight in a gorgeous collection over the loveseat. The effect was stunning.

When the client came home, he was so excited to see these pictures finally hung. Then he said, "I can't believe it. You hung them in the order of the story they tell."

That was eerie. I didn't even know they told a story. Obviously when something is right, you know it.

STEP BACK AND HAVE A LOOK

Step back and see what you've achieved. Stand in each corner of the room and look around the room, just as you did at the furniture stage. Everywhere you look, you should see art working with the furniture. The art over the mantel should look beautiful with the fireplace. It should be the right size and scale for over the mantel — not too small and not too large. The walls on both sides of the fireplace should have art that works with the art over the mantel or something else that complements the art over the mantel.

There will be art over a chest that complements it, picking up its tones and working with the theme of the chest. For example, if it is a golden-pine, country-styled chest, the art would pick up that theme, perhaps being a country landscape with brown and gold tones in it. Even the frame should be a honey-gold wood to complement the chest.

The pictures around the TV should work with the size and placement of the TV. Perhaps you've hung some black-and-whites there, or pictures with a heavy black or grey frame, depending on the TV colors you want to pick up.

You look around the room again and see the leather reading chair in the corner. Behind it is a floor lamp with a rich, cream-colored shade that complements the chocolate-brown tones of the chair. Hung over the chair near the lamp is a gorgeous landscape with cream, browns, and sage greens that bring the lamp, art, and chair together in a beautiful vignette. In fact, everywhere you look around the room you see beautiful vignettes.

Now look for the white space in the room. Is it just the right amount or are there huge expanses where you need some art, or a plant, or another piece of furniture? Perhaps one wall feels cluttered with too much art and taking away a piece feels better.

Make sure the room feels perfect just as it is. You should never require accessories to 'fix' the room. Think of accessories as if they were jewelry. You don't put on a garish outfit and then hope your jewelry will fix it. The jewelry just adds some sparkle to the outfit. Decorating your home is the same. Everything should look perfect already. The accessories just add a bit of sparkle and interest to the room; they aren't there to remedy things that are wrong. So make sure your room already looks great at this stage. It should feel like you almost don't even need accessories.

Are you there? Then it's time to accessorize!

The Art of Redesign

STEP 5 | Small Stuff

As I mentioned in the previous chapter, accessories are the jewelry in your design.

Instinctively at this stage you will want to go into the kitchen, pick out an accessory you like, and then look for a place to put it. We do that when we buy things as well. We see something we like, then bring it home and look for a place to put it. I want you to do it differently this time.

START WITH THE MANTEL

Start with the mantel again. Look at the art over the mantel and the colors in the tiles of the fireplace. Look at the space left by the art. What types of pieces would work there?

Maybe the art has a theme that you can work with.

STORIES
from Redesign

One home we did had a painting of a rowboat in whites and sage greens. We hung it over the mantel to work with the sage green in the tiles of the fireplace. We picked up the theme and colors by putting large shells that we'd found in the home on the mantel. We further picked up the theme with a bowl that was shaped and colored to look like a shell, putting it on the coffee table. A couple of books on the coffee table with the sage green color warmed up the space and further complemented our theme and the colors in the painting.

Once you decide what kind of pieces would look good on the mantel, go to your staging area to find something that would work. Pick up all the possibilities and then play with different configurations on the mantel.

If the fireplace is in the exact center of the wall in a traditional home, a symmetrical arrangement above the mantel could be best. However, in most cases asymmetrical arrangements are more pleasing to the eye. Remember to have only an odd number of items on the mantel in an asymmetrical arrangement.

Remember balance and scale. Items on the mantel must relate to the picture (or mirror) above, as with any other accessory and art. The relationship can be by theme, color, or texture. If the frame of a mirror is heavy, place a heavy accessory nearby for balance. Just remember 'like with like.'

If you don't own anything appropriate for the mantel try to find something in nature — shells, pinecones, rocks, or cut greenery. An assortment of candles usually looks nice on a mantel unless there are electric sconces above the mantel. Placing candles next to lights is redundant.

NOW ACCESSORIZE THE REST

Now look at the next space that requires accessories. Perhaps you have a dark antique table with red tones in the wood. You've hung a beautiful antique painting over it that picks up the red in the table. The painting's intricate gold frame works with the theme. Now let's put some accessories on the table to bring everything together. Look for everything you have that is gold or wooden with red tones. Also look for items with the same colors as the painting. What about some antique gold candlesticks? Perhaps some antique boxes with a similar red-toned wood and gold trim. Maybe you have a large bowl that will work. Some books with their dust jackets removed could work well with the antique theme and be used to prop up smaller items that need more height in your arrangement. Maybe you have a plant in a burnished gold pot.

Bring all the items you think will work with the painting and table into the room and start playing with them. Look at what works and what doesn't. Play with layering lots of items or keeping it simple with one or two. The accessory stage is your opportunity to have fun, so remember to be light-hearted and play.

The fine lines of this antique cabinet worked beautifully with the simply-framed picture of birds. The accessories continued the bird theme. Note the asymmetrical arrangement. Plants can work with any arrangement, but make sure the type of plant and container work with the furniture and art.

When you're finished that table, look for other places to coordinate belongings with the artwork. Maybe you have a glass table with a silver or pewter rim. You've hung a gorgeous painting with a silver or pewter frame over the table. The painting is of a beautiful woman in a flowing, light-blue dress. Now look in your staging area for all your pewter or silver pieces. Also look for anything that's light blue.

Often I'll find that in this situation the homeowner will have some female figurines in soft pastel colors that work beautifully. This is because, even over a lifetime, there tends to be a common thread in what people buy. We tend to be attracted to similar colors, shapes, or themes. I had it pointed out to me that I am drawn to circular objects. In my living room there is a built-in cabinet with a large circle cut out. I purchased an armoire for my TV that had a large brass circle in the middle. My square coffee table had a small wooden circle on each side. I had numerous round bowls and round baskets all over the room. The interesting point is that I had no idea that I was attracted to 'round.' Look for consistencies in what you are attracted to. You may be surprised by what you discover.

Accessorizing using colors that work with the furniture and art, or repeating a theme in the artwork with a collection below it creates an interesting, beautiful vignette. If you can find accessories that use the colors and the theme, the effect is spectacular.

We had a small chest that needed to take up space on a large wall. To expand it, we put the brass stand next to it, which worked well with the brass handles on the chest and visually widened it. The homeowner's silver and black art and accessories were the finishing touch. Notice how the accessories take the space where a third picture might have been hung. Use art and accessories to visually work together.

TIPS FOR ACCESSORIZING

When placing accessories, everything placed should be there for a reason. Accessories should work with the furniture and art around them. Think of picking up the color and theme of the art and the furniture so that together the furniture, art, and accessories create a beautiful vignette.

Make sure items are the correct size and scale for the surface. The weight of the pieces should be similar to the weight of the art and furniture. For example, a couple of thin crystal candlesticks would look out of place on your pine chest with the country picture hung over it. Instead, perhaps you have some heavy wooden pieces in a honey-gold color. Maybe you have a small plant that can work with them, and perhaps you have some old books in sage green and dark brown that add more warmth and interest. Books minus their book jackets are wonderful "pedestals" to elevate accessories if your accessories aren't large enough for the space.

I always find it fascinating that people own just the right art and accessories to work with the furniture. The antique radio, wallpaper, plant, art and candlesticks all give an old-world feel to this vignette.

Try to make collections of accessories as much as possible. A collection is three or more of an item — always an odd number. Look at color, theme (subject), shape and size, and function or relationship to other items, when forming collections. For example, you could have a collection of seven things that are red, or five round items of different sizes, or nine mementos of different sizes from your trip to Africa.

Think of creating triangles with your accessories (remember the rule about triangles being visually pleasing to the human eye?) Have a taller piece at one end or in the middle. Then incorporate a medium-sized piece next to it and then a smaller piece. Creating highs and lows in your arrangements adds interest and mimics the highs and lows you created throughout the room with the art and the furniture. Try to have different shapes and textures in your collection. A tall, thin piece next to a medium-sized round, thick piece, with a smaller triangular piece allows the eye to move gently from one piece to the other and adds interest.

Sometimes, though, three of exactly the same thing in different heights looks beautiful as well. Or even three, five, or seven of exactly the same thing in a row or arranged in a 'V' shape works.

Always remember that there are guidelines which are your starting point, but then you can be creative by moving away from the guideline in another direction.

Don't worry if your accessories overlap the art. Sometimes overlapping the art helps the eye look at the table, art and accessories as one vignette, tying them all together. A few leaves from a plant drifting over the art achieve this effect beautifully. Just ensure that the most important part of the artwork is still visible.

Look at the balance in your collections just as you did when you balanced the room with furniture. Put the largest in the center and fan out from there; put the tallest piece in the back and shortest in the front. Reduce the height in groupings gradually just like you do with furniture. Make size reductions by thirds so that the second is two-thirds of the first, the third is two-thirds of the second, and so forth.

If you have a collection of many small pieces, it's very difficult to find a spot where they are the right scale. Sometimes you can unify them by using a tray. You can also place a few on top of books laid flat in a bookcase, so that they aren't lost.

One of my favorite ways to display small collections is with a wall-hung curio cabinet. The shelves are small so that the items take up about two-thirds of the space. Also, you can walk up to them at eye level and look at each piece individually. The whole curio cabinet becomes a colorful piece of art and the collection can be seen and appreciated.

Use small plants as if they were accessories. They provide wonderful texture to almost any collection. Even plants have different styles and themes, though. Put your jade plant with your Oriental pieces, your palm with your brightly colored tropical art, and your feathery fern with your antique pieces.

Whenever possible, put round with round and square with square; that is, a round lamp base on a round table and a square one on the square table, or an oval dish on an oval coffee table. Although I find that sometimes the opposite is interesting too. Remember that rules can be broken!

Instinctively we tend to want to balance everything: three pieces on the left and three pieces on the right. Think of doing asymmetrical arrangements instead. Lean toward the heavy side; e.g. if you have one odd piece left over for an arrangement on a mantel or table, place it on the more weighted side. A great look is to have one large item on one side of a table or mantel balanced by three items of differing heights on the other side.

Mix textures. Be careful not to use only glass or porcelain objects. Try to find wicker, greenery, or fabric to blend in with other accessories. You can add texture to a room with area rugs, plates, sculptures, throws, textiles, baskets, wall reliefs, and sconces. If you have a runner or beautiful cloth, consider draping it over one side of a table instead of covering the whole table, so the beautiful wood of the table can be seen as well.

Keep some white space. Do not overfill the tabletops; leave some space so the tables have an actual function if needed for the occasional beverage. Keep all windowsills clutter free unless you have a very deep bay window. If you display a collection on the coffee table, consider keeping the end tables free. Avoid putting several items on a small end table that already holds a large lamp. They will look out of scale.

DECORATING COFFEE TABLES

The arrangement on a coffee table should be simple and fairly dramatic. If the table is elaborately carved, it may be preferable to leave it alone. Also, if you have a lot of accessories on the side tables, it's nice to leave the coffee table empty.

Tall pieces on the coffee table are fine but only if they don't create a hindrance to conversation. Just as in any arrangement, use one item, a pair of items, or a collection of items (odd numbers only).

Some possibilities for coffee tables:

✳ a piece of sculpture or an interesting bowl

✳ candlesticks or a medium-to-tall vase with fresh flowers or greenery

✳ two or three interesting boxes

✳ attractive books

BOOKCASES

Bookcases are a challenge in most homes. How do we make them look good as well as house our books?

Consider the theme and look of the entire room when designing your bookcases. Open space between large objects works well on contemporary shelving whereas lots of books and ornaments, with a few small plants, give a warm look to a more traditional setting.

Think in terms of themes when you design a bookcase. Sometimes your theme will just be "all books." Or the theme could be "books with wooden objects" or "books with earth-toned objects." If you have a large collection of something such as ornaments of horses, perhaps your theme is horses. In that case you could have books, your horse collection, and even pictures of horses in the bookcase.

If you don't have enough objects to 'theme' the entire bookcase, then try to at least keep the same theme within each shelf.

If you have a lot of books, then removing their dust jackets and filling up every shelf with them gives a nice, clean look. Bring the books out to the edge of the shelf, leaving only an inch in front of them. Then make sure all the spines are lined up across the front. This will look better than pushing the books to the back of the shelf and will also prevent you from placing objects in front of the books, which just looks cluttered.

Organize your books so that you can find what you want easily. It makes the most sense to keep books by subject area: novels, travel books, gardening books, etc. Within those categories, organizing them by height with the tallest on the left, right, or center of a shelf creates a simple pattern for the eye. Books don't have to be arranged from tallest to shortest within each shelf. Try shelving them so that the tops of the spines form a pleasing gradually curved line.

Keeping the largest books on the bottom shelves lets them act as a visual 'foundation' for the rest of the books. Taller books can be laid on their side, adding visual interest. Paperbacks are not as attractive as hardcover books so put these in a family room or bedroom rather than your living room if possible.

If you have space in your bookshelves, vary books with interesting objects to create dimension and add pockets of color to the shelves and the room. Remember to think in terms of themes. Objects can include a well-framed family photo, a souvenir from a trip, a beautiful bowl, basket or ornament, or even a small plant or vase of greenery.

There are a few different ways to include objects on your bookshelves.

1. You could have one or two shelves that have only one, two, or three beautiful objects in them and no books. Choose shelves at eye level for the most impact.

2. Create a pattern for the eye to follow from top to bottom by alternating the placement of objects with books in a zigzag pattern. Remember that diagonals and triangles are attractive to the eye. For example, the top shelf could have books on the left and a single object on the right. The second shelf could have a single object on the left and books on the right. Continue this pattern to the bottom. If you have two bookshelves side by side,

fill the top left shelf with books and put interesting objects on the top right shelf. Put interesting objects on the second left shelf and books on the second right shelf. Keep repeating to the bottom of the two bookcases.

ZIGZAG

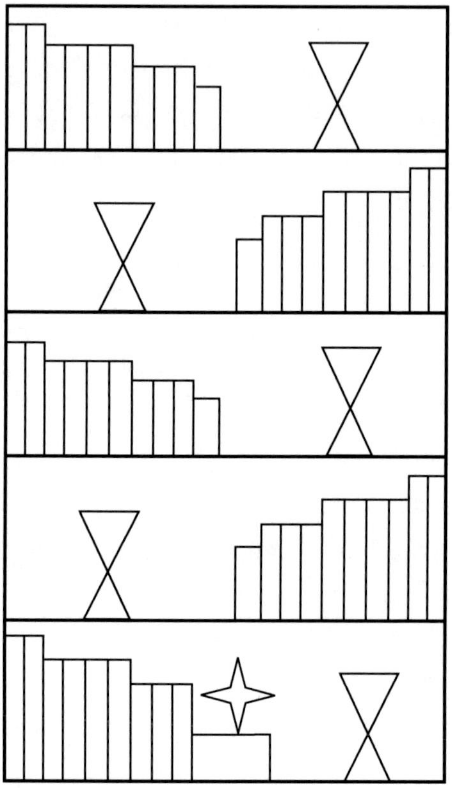

3. Use the patterns from #2 above but lay some of the books down for interest. Occasionally add an intriguing object on the top of these 'fallen' books.

The Art of Redesign

4. Follow a "centering" pattern as in the diagram below. On each shelf, something is centered. Perhaps it is just one item, or maybe three items. Perhaps it is one item centered between books, or just books centered on a shelf.

CENTERED

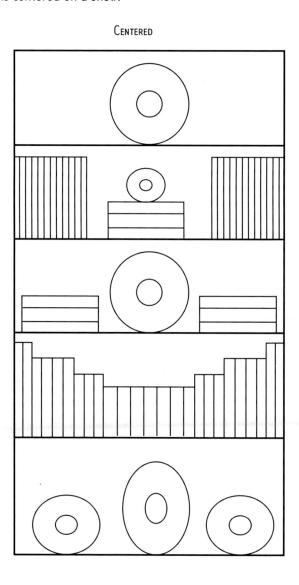

5. If you have two bookshelves side by side, try the 'mirror image' format. Each bookcase shelf is the mirror image of the same shelf on the bookcase beside it.

MIRROR IMAGE

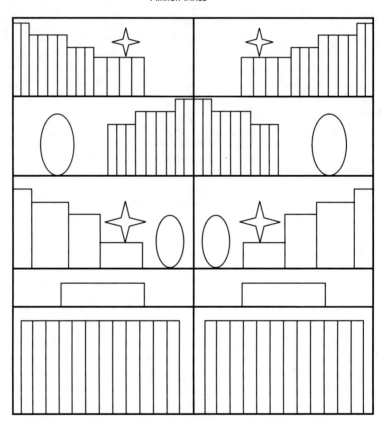

6. For a single bookcase, you can try the 'balanced' format. Every shelf has something in the center that is 'balanced' by two similar things on either side. For example, a vase in the middle of a shelf can be balanced by books on either side, or by two smaller vases on either side.

BALANCED

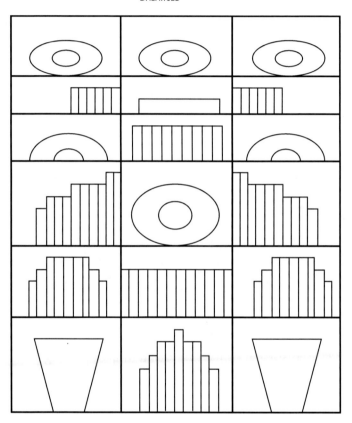

Carol had some built-in glass shelves that had troubled her from the day she moved into her home. She could never find accessories that worked. Part of the problem was that the shelves were quite narrow. The only solution she could come up with was to use small items. Unfortunately they were out of scale with the shelves. The result was just a bunch of tiny things on shelves that had about a foot of space between them. Ideally you would use two-thirds of the height of the shelf in your arrangements.

We chose a theme of natural and wooden objects for the shelves, putting three artfully designed wooden bowls her brother had made on stands so they could fit on the shelves. We then arranged the bowls in a triangle on the shelves, placing two pictures with frames of similar wood to offset them. We incorporated some rocks, twigs, and other items from nature to complete our design.

Carol couldn't believe it. Not only had we created artful arrangements on her shelves, but her favorite bowls and art were now also prominently displayed so she and her guests could appreciate them.

Here are a few more tips for bookcases:

✳ Group smaller objects to create impact but beware of the fine line between clustered and cluttered.

✳ Create symmetrical groupings within the overall composition, e.g. two taller objects on either side of a low, wide bowl.

✳ Shelves filled with books from end to end look best at the bottom of the display; otherwise the bookcase will appear top-heavy.

✳ Create more interest on shelves by varying the heights of the shelves themselves.

✳ Remove one of the shelves and hang a picture or mirror to provide an unexpected touch.

✹ Look at hanging pictures, ornaments, baskets, masks, etc. in the back of open-backed bookcases to work with the accessories.

When you're done, step back and look at the whole bookcase. Is there anything that bothers you? If so, change it. When you decide that it looks good, then it does. Your eye will always tell you when something is out of balance, or doesn't fit, or is the wrong height. Just trust your instincts.

CHINA CABINETS

If you love your china cabinet, or need it for storage, then let's enhance its beauty and make it useful.

Many people put all their china in the bottom of their china cabinet and display the glasses and crystal in the top. Over time, other items get added to the top of the china cabinet because it's an easy place to store something. Before long, it's a jumble of items. The irony is that the bottom space (which no one sees) is quite neat and tidy, with all the china stacked.

I'd like to suggest a novel idea. Let's move the china to the top, along with the glasses we use all the time. The rest of the items, which we don't use that often, can go in the bottom.

Interestingly enough, I find that the color in a client's china tends to work with the art we've hung in the dining room. Remember earlier in the book when I talked about the common thread, where people tend to be attracted to similar colors, shapes, or themes even over a lifetime? That concept is definitely at work in this area.

Here's a simple formula you can follow for a standard china cabinet with two shelves and three sections.

Let's do the center section of the china cabinet first.

1. Place a row of cups and saucers on the top shelf.

2. Place three to five plates on plate stands behind the cups and saucers (or just stand them in the little groove that's often in the wood of the shelf).

3. Stack the remainder of the plates and the bowls on the bottom shelf. This makes them so easy to access that you'll be using your 'good' china all the time.

4. Place a large, matching or complementary casserole or dish on the middle shelf. For interest, add a figurine, a vase, a teapot, or something comparable in color or texture that complements the china.

BEFORE: *Most people put all their glass and crystal in the top of the china cabinet. The result is often a cluttered look without a lot of color.*

AFTER: *If you like your china and use it, then putting your china on the top and the lesser-used crystal items in the bottom makes sense. I'm surprised by how often the art in the dining room works with the china. The cabinet then becomes another wall of art. Note how easy it is to take your plates out of the cabinet.*

Now let's do the sides of the cabinet. This is where you display all your stemware. Straight rows of stemware on either side of your colorful china will create a simple 'frame' for the center of the cabinet. When you have the doors open, it's tempting to offset the stemware to make it look 'pretty.' However, when you close the doors, it will just look jumbled because of all the glass reflection. Instead, just line them up, putting 'like with like.'

If the china cabinet is white (or a light wood), try not to display glass or silver. Colored china or other decorative items are far more dramatic. The only time crystal and silver work especially well in a china cabinet is when they are displayed against beautifully colored or dark-grained wood.

BEFORE: *Remember that anything behind glass can be seen. Items behind glass need to be designed, not just stored. This is a common sight in most of the glass cabinets I see.*

AFTER: *Look at the difference you can make. Think about having a consistent theme and putting like items together. Items can be grouped by color, by theme, by shape, or by their functional relationship to each other.*

Try not to put too much in the cabinet. If you must because you need the storage, line up pieces by color and size so that there is a strict uniform look. Uniformity can be the design.

> Tip for silver: Save the silica packages that come with shoes and other packaged goods. Put them in the silver to keep humidity out and slow tarnishing. You don't need to polish silver for hours anymore. There are numerous recipes for cleaning silver on the Internet.

HOMES WITH SMALL CHILDREN

I've noticed that there are two types of parents when it comes to home décor. There are those who are determined to have an adult-looking home and who train their children not to touch breakables. Then there are those who put all their breakables up high or in closets until their children are a little older and let their children just play.

If you are in the second category, you can still have an attractive home. In a home where a toddler lives, use toys to decorate the family room coffee table or end tables. Use children's books on the coffee table, a dinosaur on the end table, a child's rocker in a corner, fake plants that can be knocked over without spilling dirt. In the living room decorate with unbreakable items. Use interesting baskets, wooden bowls, colored fabric, driftwood. There are numerous items that are both safe for small children and attractive. Just be creative.

You're done! You've placed just the right kind of accessories to work with the art and the furniture. Everywhere you look there are beautiful vignettes. No matter where someone is sitting in the room, they have something beautiful to look at — and you created it!

When I redesign someone's home, usually people are thrilled immediately. But sometimes you or some of your family members may not like it right away. Change can be hard for some people. Occasionally clutter helps people feel safe, or they're just not used to living without it. Even if some of your family members don't like it right away it's important to just leave your newly redesigned home intact for about two weeks. This will ensure that any negativity isn't just a reaction to change. After that, if there's anything that they still want changed, go for it.

BEFORE: *This family had small toddlers so everything had been put away and placed up high.*

AFTER: *We decorated the room with toys and children's books which gave much-needed color and life to the room.*

I had one client who didn't like her redesign immediately. I asked her to just wait for about two weeks and that if she still didn't like it after that time, I would work with her until she did. After a week and a half she called me. "I'm finally starting to see how you highlighted everything I love in my home," she said. Sometimes it just takes a while to get used to change.

The Art of Redesign is all about creating a space that works for you, that highlights what you love, and gives you a look and feel in your home that reflects you, your family, your passions, and your loves. Those are the basics of beautiful. When you create that type of space, you have a home.

Postscript

HIRING A PROFESSIONAL

If you are a busy person who doesn't have time to go through this process yourself, you may want to hire someone to do it for you. You may also just not have an interest in doing it yourself and would rather just go out for the day and come home to your 'new' home. Or you may decide that your creative self prefers a different venue rather than redesigning your home.

That's when you may want to hire a professional, as this couple did.

STORIES
from Redesign

We redesigned the home of Selina and Faisal, who had just been married. They had a number of nice things but the home just wasn't coming together. The dining room was small and the living room felt crowded with the large furniture they had purchased. They wanted a home they could be proud of but didn't know how to make that happen.

The first thing we did was to shift the living room furniture in this open-plan space so that it was further away from the dining room. This allowed us to turn the dining room table horizontally, creating a much larger dining room area. We also angled the bookcases at the end of the living room so that we could angle an upholstered chair in front of one of them.

Rather than have the large sofa face the fireplace where it was cutting off the flow of the room, we put it perpendicular to the fireplace where it divided the living room and dining room. We then put their large chair-and-a-half facing the fireplace (and, incidentally, their plasma TV which was mounted over the mantel). The effect was to create a square living room with a cozy conversation area, rather than a long narrow space. The overall feel was that the living room was more spacious and open, just by the way we placed the furniture.

The couple had small pictures of friends and themselves all over the living room. I suggested that they buy 12 identical small black frames and that we could do a collection on the wall. We arranged the collection beside one of the bookcases and were able to hang 12 photos in a very small area. This not only got rid of all the clutter of the photos, but the photos were hung in a spot where you could easily walk up to them and look at them. They were now a great conversation piece.

One of our challenges was that the couple still wanted to display their guest book, wedding album, and other wedding paraphernalia. However the items were too ornate and were the wrong colors for the room. They also didn't lend themselves to the contemporary, clean look that the couple wanted. We had put a sofa table behind the loveseat with room to walk behind it to look out the window. By arranging all their wedding items on the sofa table we were able to hide them from view but still make them easily accessible. When you walked behind the loveseat, you looked at a beautiful collection of wedding memorabilia.

When the clients came home they were absolutely thrilled. Selina was particularly cute. Her response went something like: "Oh my god! Oh my god!" Then she would look in another direction and say, "Oh my god!" At one point she said, "All I seem to be able to say is 'Oh my god.'" Then she looked in another direction and said "Oh my god!" After she had seen the room, we took her behind the loveseat. Tears came into her eyes as she saw all her wedding memories beautifully displayed on the table. "I knew these didn't look right in the room but it was so important to me to have them out," she said. "This is perfect."

———————————

REDESIGN VERSUS TRADITIONAL DESIGN

There are many great decorators and interior designers in the world, gifted and trained to help you renovate your home, buy draperies and new furniture, and help you choose colors. A redesigner, however, will create the best home possible, working with your existing furnishings. Once your redesign is done, you will confidently know what needs to be purchased, how big it should be, what color it should be, and where it will go. This ensures that you don't make costly mistakes buying something you don't really need, or spending a lot of money on something that doesn't work.

Trained interior redesigners know how to ask all the right questions. They will be able to determine how to make your home reflect you. They will find out what you love and highlight it. They will make the home functional for you and your family. All that's required is your time, for about an hour, to tour them through your home and answer their questions.

Most important, a trained redesigner will do everything for you in one day. While they're doing that, you can be at a spa, having coffee with friends, or taking your children to the park. You come home at the end of the day and it's all done.

 STORIES
from Redesign

I've had client's spouses say that it's a lot of money for "just moving furniture around."

One man in particular was against the whole idea. He didn't want to spend the money; he didn't want his television moved; and he was convinced it was a waste of time. His wife talked him into doing it anyway (after numerous negotiations). When he came home after the redesign, he couldn't believe it. "I love this," he said. "I never thought it was possible to create such a difference by just moving things around."

I had another client who 'let us' do the redesign just as a gift to his wife. He was content with his home the way it was but wanted her to be happy. When they came home at the end of the day I couldn't decide which of them was more excited. He was particularly thrilled by how we'd highlighted his favorite pieces of art. They looked fabulous.

But here's the best part. When his wife got home, she said, "I've spent the whole day shopping for a new china cabinet because this one didn't work in the space. I don't need to buy one now. You made this one work! You just saved me $5000!" I turned to the husband and he smiled.

Another time we did a large home of a couple who had just moved in and were having trouble arranging their furnishings in their new home. They had a huge living room and put all their sofas in one large seating area. The result was that you couldn't have a conversation in the room because the sofas were so far apart. Also, the TV was an uncomfortable distance away. We were able to create two different areas in the room: one for watching the television, and another for conversation.

Across from the huge fireplace was a bank of windows the length of the room, facing the garden. Instead of the traditional sofa table behind the sofa that was facing the fireplace, we had arranged two wing-back chairs and a table, looking out at the garden.

When the wife got home, she was thrilled. She couldn't wait for her husband to get home from his business trip. Unfortunately, when he got home he was tired, slightly irritable, and not pleased with having to face "any kind of change." The next morning, however, he got his paper and sat down in one of the wing-back chairs overlooking the garden. After a few moments he looked up at his wife and smiled. "This is nice," he said.

FINDING THE RIGHT REDESIGNER

So how to find the redesigner that's right for you?

In Canada, you can go to the Canadian Redesigners Association website at www.canadianredesigners.org.

In the US, you can go to the Interior Redesign Industry Specialists website at www.WeRedesign.com.

All the redesigners listed on these sites have been specifically trained to do a makeover of your home using your existing furnishings. Find one in your location. Give a few of them a call to see which one you feel a connection with on the phone. Then hire that person to do a consultation. Even at that point, make sure you feel comfortable with them. Do they listen to you? Are they taking notes? Do you have a sense that they truly care about creating the best home possible for you and your family?

Trust your instincts. You will know if this is the right person for you or not. If not, try another redesigner. If it is, then book a day for the redesign and prepare to be amazed with the results.

Yes, even your home can be spectacularly different. I've had clients tell me that they really didn't think I could do anything with their home and their things. Somehow they felt like what they owned just wasn't 'good enough.' They were astounded at the difference after the redesign.

BEFORE *Beautiful things lose their impact if they're not placed properly.*

AFTER *Help your home to be the best it can possibly be.*

I've had clients tell me that they constantly move their furniture around. They've tried everything and don't believe that we can come up with anything that will work. They were astounded at the transformations.

You've reached the end of this book, probably after a quick, initial read to decide whether it's something you can do on your own or not. Regardless of whether you do it yourself or hire a professional, remember you can transform your present home using the possessions you already have. You really can.

You can create a haven and enhance your life — and you don't have to buy anything new.

Acknowledgements

There are so many people who helped me with this book.

My heartfelt thanks to:

✵ My first editor, Michael Kaye, who got me started and gave me the confidence to proceed.

✵ Jim Osborne, who edited the majority of the book, and gave it structure. His enthusiasm gave me a lot of confidence.

✵ Christine Frank who caught so many of those little grammatical errors.

✵ Toolbox Creative for the amazing design of the cover and the interior.

✵ Hellen Buttigieg, for her encouragement and wonderful foreword.

✵ Barbara Graham, Sandi Gerrard, Joanne Hatherly, and Waheeda Harris who were kind enough to read the book and give me their comments and testimonials.

✵ Gail Richards, who helped me brainstorm titles and gave me marketing advice.

✵ Jan King who convinced me I had a book worth printing and encouraged me throughout the process.

✵ Dan Curtis, who read the book and gave me his comments.

✵ Wayne Kelly, who taught me about radio interviews.

✵ Michael Port and The Product Factory.

* All the talented women who took my redesign and home staging classes, contributing their talent and expertise to creating the redesigns featured in the book.

* All the generous people who trusted me with their homes and gave me permission to use their stories and their photos.

* My parents, and my mother-in-law and friend, Barb, who are my biggest fans.

* And finally, my husband Tony who provides me with the support that allows me to pursue my passions.

* Anyone else who helped me and should have been mentioned, but whose name I forgot, my sincere apologies.

156

The Art *of* Redesign

158

The Art of Redesign